Praise for Awaken Visionary Voice

If there's one thing I know, ...
visionary voices in the world and with this magical
book, Leah is holding space for that to happen.
Awakening the Visionary Voice guides you through a
powerful unfolding, so you can be more fully
expressed (and write from that place). I'm so
grateful to Leah for the work she's doing in the
world and the visionary voices that will be activated
after reading this book!

Nicola Humber,
founder of The Unbound Press

Awakening the Visionary Voice is a call to freedom
and self-trust. Leah gently guides us through
unraveling our social conditioning to tap into our
visionary voice inside as a revolutionary act. If
you've ever felt like you're "too much," this book is
for you.

Megan Winkler, MBA,
founder of The Good Business Witch

Awakening the Visionary Voice was like coming home to myself. Finally, permission and gentle invitations on how to access and write from the most essential parts of ourselves. Leah's book is accessible, immediately applicable, and revolutionary.

Laura Shaw, author of
Unveiling the Tarot

Reading *Awakening the Visionary Voice* felt like every word was giving permission for my soul and voice to come alive. Because of Leah's work, I not only feel capable but believe we all have a path, and a story to tell. I know this is the book you need to guide you down your path.

Dana Olivo, coach & host of the
Reconnecting with Pleasure podcast

Leah's book, *Awakening the Visionary Voice*, takes you on an empowering journey of opening your heart and growing your capacity for self-expression. This is a must read for anyone who wants to find, clarify, or amplify their unique voice in the world. Leah's words are as grounding as they are a call to step up into your full power.

Isabelle McKusick Marantz,
founder of Arrived Retreats

AWAKENING
the
VISIONARY VOICE

Also by Leah Kent

Intuitive Moon Rituals

Sanctuary

AWAKENING

the

VISIONARY VOICE

*Writing and creative wisdom to unlock
your most powerful self-expression*

LEAH KENT

creator of Wild Embodied Writing

wildmoonpress.com

For the wild wisdom keepers -
there is no such thing as too much of you

CONTENTS

You Are a Visionary - 1

UNFOLDING AND UNFURLING – 3

ACCESSING THE INNER WELL – 11

A SHORT NOTE ON WRITING – 17

UNPREDICTABLE AWAKENING – 19

The Visionary Voice - 25

TRUST – 27

FREEDOM – 47

PLEASURE – 59

CLARITY – 79

COURAGE – 93

INTUITION – 109

BOUNDARIES – 123

ENOUGHNESS – 147

Integration - 165

ACKNOWLEDGMENTS – 177

ABOUT THE AUTHOR – 179

YOU ARE A
VISIONARY

———————

You have everything you need to

bring your sacred work to life

UNFOLDING AND UNFURLING

You're here because you are a visionary in a constant state of unfolding and unfurling. Whether through words, song, healing touch, or holding space for others, you have answered a pull deep within you to make a life of meaning. You know that anything and everything you do can nurture the universal principles of love, light, connection, and joy.

Even if you call yourself a teacher, healer, guide, or coach, you see yourself as a writer. You share your wisdom with words, often through a mix of speaking and writing. A creative impulse exists within you that yearns to birth things. You know you're here to launch bold projects, initiate change-making missions, contribute to the reimagination of new systems, or lead intimate transformational experiences.

To fully embody this calling as a heart-centered visionary, you realize the necessity of developing an authentic, powerful voice. You know how important it is to communicate your ideas with words and language that represent your true self, connect with others, and breathe life into your vision.

The world is waiting for you to claim this birthright. Perhaps more than ever, we must speak up so we can find one another to bring a new reality into being. You have a gift to contribute to the unraveling of an entire spectrum of fractured ideologies in our culture that cause harm to so many human beings.

You've heard the call, you feel the pull, and now is the time to answer. Now is the time to share the wisdom you've gathered, reclaimed, and cultivated.

Within each of us is a visionary voice waiting to be liberated and awakened. I don't believe that being a visionary is reserved for a few genetically lucky or chosen souls in each generation. I reject the idea that only a handful of us are granted exclusive access to a source of remarkable insight and divine inspiration.

What if we are all born visionaries?

What if the ability to access a flow of creative possibility and bring your ideas into tangible form is a universal gift of the human experience?

How can we actively cultivate, practice, and hone our ability to embody this visionary nature and express ourselves through the power of our voice and the written word?

First, let's establish what I mean by the word visionary, and peer beneath its surface. Our journey will be more fruitful if we pause to understand the energy, meaning, and roots of this concept.

According to the Oxford English Dictionary, a visionary is any of the following:

1. thinking about or planning the future with imagination or wisdom

2. relating to or having the ability to see visions in a dream or trance, or as a supernatural apparition

3. a person with original ideas about what the future will or could be like

Just notice how broad these definitions are. There's not a single reference to this being an exclusive or rare quality. Anyone can tap into this ability to engage with the future, to receive visions, and generate original ideas about what's to come.

Once you accept yourself as a visionary, you have another question to sit with. How will you express your ideas with the world?

For most of us, we eventually reach a point where we feel deeply compelled to stop hiding our truth. There's a ripening taking place within us until we realize we'll simply burst if we don't start sharing what we know with others.

This happened for me, and I imagine if you've picked up this book, you have an idea what I'm describing. You've walked a particular winding path and gathered wisdom, skills, and fresh insights along the way. They nourish you and your loved ones on an intimate level, because you've applied them to your life.

While you may bring them to the work you do, you can't ignore the desire to create a more meaningful way of sharing what you've learned with a broader community. Or perhaps you want to let go of the ho-hum work you've been doing, so you have more time, space, and energy to do more of what lights a fire within you.

It's exhausting to water down your opinions while you yearn for something more. You begin to wonder: what happens next?

You're feeling the call of your visionary voice. It's asking you to wake up and share your gifts with others. To leave a legacy, to weave your thread into the tapestry of human wisdom, growth, and evolution. The time has come to harvest your fertile ideas and share the bounty with others.

Despite the call and growing sense of urgency to express your ideas into the world, you may encounter resistance, fear, and obstacles along the way.

This push and pull between desire and resistance is how I arrived at this gathering of Creative Visionary Truths. Slowly yet steadily, I answered the call to express my voice and discovered ways to dissolve, release, and alchemize the many blocks that stood in my path.

My work is not yet done, and I don't believe it ever will be. I'll always have more fear to dissolve and more wisdom to share. I accept that this dance is ongoing, because growth and expansion are the only constants in this embodied human experience.

What you hold in your hands is my heartfelt offering, based on what I've gathered over decades of self-study and interconnected explorations. These are the visionary truths that have sustained me while honoring my calling and fulfilling my commitment to sharing what I learn along the way.

What I invite you try on before you immerse yourself in this work are these core beliefs:

CREATIVE VISIONARY TRUTHS

- You are equipped with a direct channel to the realm of creative consciousness.

- You have access to a limitless flow of inspiration and abundance.

- You have the ability to manifest your visions, dreams, and desires in a tangible form.

- You feel called to create meaning with your life and work.

- Everything you do is driven by a desire for love and connection.

- You have everything you need to bring your sacred work to life.

I believe these visionary qualities are stitched right into the fabric of our being. These desires and abilities are seeds that have been planted in your heart and are intended to blossom throughout a lifetime of love, connection, and creative living.

ACCESSING THE INNER WELL

How would it feel if you allowed the visionary voice within you to be expressed and heard? Can you pin-point its source? Do you know where this calling is located within you?

Imagine that your visionary voice exists in a luscious courtyard with a bubbling fountain of cool, clear water at its center. Surrounding this fountain are a number of doorways, all pointing directly at this flow of energy.

This fountain is the outlet for the creative river within you, a deep aquifer of wisdom and words you can access at all times. Whenever you need to visit this source, you can walk through any one of these doorways. No matter how you find your way here, you'll be delivered to this rich, verdant, and nourishing center.

Personally, I resonate with calling this my inner sanctuary, but you can find your own words for this realm. You may already have an image of what this creative source looks like, how it sounds, or how it feels. It could be a glowing stone in the middle of a mossy forest floor, or a cloud that pulses with electricity and sends out purple sparks.

The landscape and surroundings will be as unique as you are. They may be real or imagined. Regardless of the details, your invitation throughout this book is to wake up to this source, which animates your visionary voice.

Everyone finds their own way to this inner source; the pathways are as infinite and unique as each of us. This is a journey of reconnection, remembering, and reclaiming. You are born with a direct and unencumbered link to this source.

You are pure spirit, walking the earth in a human body. Then life swoops in and we're told in this way and that to sever our healthy connection to our true selves and the ground beneath our feet. We receive a clear, albeit unspoken, message to hide it, ignore it, or suppress it. Until the time comes that you are called to return and retrace your steps back here.

There are no right or wrong ways to awaken your visionary voice and begin expressing yourself in real life. But over time, I've found a few beacons that are reliably universal at leading to this inner wisdom. Within these pages, you'll be guided to explore these qualities, try them on, and discover how you can use them to access and strengthen your own visionary voice.

Let me clarify what I mean by a *quality*. I use this particular term because it goes beyond actions and practices. A quality is intangible; it's the nature of a thing or an idea. It's the energy of a particular concept. To embody a quality is to find outlets to express it in tangible or physical ways.

Voices are like this too; they have an energy to them and a wholeness that exists below the surface of the words being spoken. The quality of a voice is present whether you're actively speaking or enjoying a moment of silence. We can translate these same qualities of our voice from our minds into a string of words that we commit to the page in written form.

It takes commitment, courage, and resilience to acknowledge, let alone express, the full power of your voice. Too many of us give up on this pursuit, and our creative gifts become calcified and trapped within us.

Though it may feel uncomfortable to honor and speak your truth, it's equally uncomfortable, if not more so, to suppress this wisdom within yourself.

As you move through these pages, I invite you to embrace a spirit of curiosity and an open heart. Awakening the visionary voice is a journey of self-discovery and awareness, not a prescription or a method. You can dip in and out of these qualities and find the one you most need in a given moment.

The Visionary Qualities

TRUST: trusting ourselves first

FREEDOM: releasing our limiting attachments

PLEASURE: allowing joy and delight to be our guidance system

CLARITY: opening to the cycle of certainty and mystery

COURAGE: greeting resistance with an open heart

INTUITION: following your inner compass

BOUNDARIES: honoring your time, attention, and energy

ENOUGHNESS: living from self-love and contentment

There is a chapter dedicated to each of these qualities, inviting you to look at how it shows up in your creative life. You can read this book from start to finish, or take the non-linear approach of moving from one idea to another in any order that pleases you.

Some of these topics aren't what you'd expect to find in a book about creativity and writing. Being a visionary is who you are, it's more than what you do or what you create. It's impossible to separate your ideas, your art, and your daily life when you're called to this path of big self-expression.

For myself, a mother, working writer, and book coach, I need my whole life to be organized in a way that nourishes my creativity and fuels my voice. I have to choose enoughness every day, set and maintain healthy boundaries, and renew my commitment to trusting myself from moment to moment.

These threads can't be pulled and picked apart without leaving the fabric of your life weakened and threadbare. Your voice can't shine or soar when you're stuck in a tangled web of creative resistance.

If you're anything like me, you thrive when you feel connected to yourself, your voice, and other creative kindred spirits. Through these pages, we can wake up together and help one another find the way.

You have something to say and wisdom to share. Your voice is yearning to be awakened, liberated, and amplified. And you've got books, businesses, and change-making movements within you that the world is ready and waiting to experience.

A SHORT NOTE
ON WRITING

This is a writing book, but I use that term loosely. Writing has always helped me access my inner voice, but it's only one way to approach the ideas in this book. In my personal experience, writing with pen and paper allows me to slow down, breathe, and find my own flow and rhythm with my words.

But each of us needs to honor what works best. So, by all means, write in a way that feels good. Record voice notes if you want or type the words out. The point is to consciously develop an outlet for your voice, a conduit for that visionary energy to flow through you and out into the world.

While there are dedicated writing prompts to support your inner exploration of these qualities, any of these ideas can become sparks for self-reflection. If you're looking for guidance on developing a writing practice, this is a brief roundup of my best advice:

- Write as often as you reliably and comfortably can.

- Always keep a journal nearby to capture snippets of inspiration.

- Talk to yourself when you're alone or in the shower, then go write it down.

- When you feel yourself drifting off while writing, use the phrase "what I really mean is" and then start writing again.

- If we can say there's a goal for a writing practice, it's simply to get at the heart of who you are, what you believe in, and what is true for you.

- Write for yourself first, without self-judgment, self-consciousness or criticism.

UNPREDICTABLE AWAKENING

At the age of 25, I quit my life completely and embarked on a grand adventure of discovery and healing. I had the feeling I was living someone else's life and hoped I could figure out a way to get back to my own. I didn't know what that was supposed to look like, but I never stopped believing it was there.

I resigned from my job, broke up with my boyfriend, sold all my belongings, and hit the restart button. Then I traveled, first to the Ukraine and then to Vietnam. Three months into this self-imposed state of shock, I landed on the Big Island of Hawaii, which turned out to be the perfect place to rediscover myself and the truth of my visionary self.

When I look back at this awakening, I'm so proud of 25-year-old Leah for mustering up the courage and resolve to take this leap of faith. I had been drifting towards a misaligned future, but my wise inner woman wasn't having any of that.

She started roaring and sending up flares to get my attention. It came in the form of broken bones and being passed over for job promotions. It came as synchronicity and divine coincidence and visitations from fierce hawks and aggressive seagulls.

My soul had something to say, and she was persistent. She never stopped her warnings, love notes and reminders, waiting for those moments when I was either hopeless or happy enough to hear her.

As I tuned in and took notice, it dawned on me that everywhere I turned, the message was clear:

You must stop avoiding the truth

You're here for a reason

You have something to share

It's time to do what you're here to do

In the years since that first rupture, I took the idea more seriously that I could tap into a higher consciousness as a source of guidance, spiritual nourishment, and insight. I finally questioned why I was forever trying to force myself to fit into a culture that wasn't meant for me.

When this book first started to reveal itself to me, I was working deeply with the idea of Shakti, the Sanskrit word that translates roughly to 'divine feminine creative power.'

I was excited to work with such a potent energy, but quickly second-guessed my decision to take on such a big concept. Doubts bounced around in my head like:

Who do I think I am to step into this kind of power? I just know someone's going to tell me I'm doing this all wrong.

Here I go again, leaping towards something dangerous without planning ahead.

Surely this is the sort of thing I need permission for or can only obtain through a very official and expensive spiritual training.

Just being with this cacophony of thoughts, I saw how this is exactly what keeps most of us feeling small and powerless. Almost immediately after one of these intrusive, negative thoughts emerged, I could feel how false these ideas were that tried to convince me I needed permission from outside of myself to awaken my visionary voice and step into my true radiance.

This is what I finally understood, that I hope to share with others: You do not need permission to be your most authentic, powerful self.

No one needs to give you a signed certificate before you unleash your full creative force into the world. When you're glowing with your own truth, you'll have a clarity of mind, wisdom of surrender, and an open channel to receive inspiration that guides you to make the impact on the world you long for.

Your visionary flame is already lit, just waiting to be stoked and nourished with the oxygen it needs to rise up in a beautiful blaze of fierce love and creative inspiration. As you write and deepen your connection to your visionary voice, this light will grow and grow, illuminating you from the inside out.

I want to validate what you already know to be true: you are an absolute miracle. Right now is the perfect moment to expand your vision of what's possible for yourself and your life. If you're reading these words, it's because you're ready to tap into your visionary self, the part of you who is ready to speak up, be seen, and share your brilliant, visionary ideas with a world that is very much waiting for them.

THE
VISIONARY
VOICE

Reclaim, remember, awaken

TRUST

It's a bold claim to say that trusting yourself is a revolution, but for many of us, there's no better way to frame it. Being a human being is vulnerable! We need other people. We need to fit in and belong to the web of community to secure our own survival.

Without a healthy reciprocity with others, we are banished, isolated, and left to wither. This is a dramatic way of expressing it, but this is how it feels to our delicate nervous systems. We adapt to the world around us, donating portions of our trust to others in order to maintain our belonging.

Most of us end up carrying a basic rule that sounds a bit like: "trust myself and be banished, trust everyone else and stay safe."

Sadly, the healthy reciprocity of true belonging is warped in modern culture. It's harder and harder to find functioning social ecosystems where we can safely or confidently place that level of trust in the hands of another. You end up losing yourself to a system that doesn't give back what you deserve. The exchange is draining, and you're left with less than you had to begin with.

In the realm of writing and self-expression, this turns up as suppressing, doubting, or silencing your own voice. To belong to the crowd, you decide to keep your thoughts to yourself. You learn it isn't safe to speak up, shine brightly, or draw attention to yourself.

No wonder we walk around with a deep wounding that keeps us biting our tongues and avoiding confrontation.

When visionaries start speaking up and telling the truth, feathers can get ruffled. This is why it's such a revolutionary act to trust yourself, reclaim your voice, and start sharing your story. From where you stand, this flow of self-expression is a way to cultivate power, strength, and joy.

When you are centered in compassion, kindness, and integrity, it feels amazing to tell people what you really feel, what you believe, and what you stand for. But there are fewer and fewer places where it feels safe to do this. Which brings us to an important truth in this revolution:

The problem isn't YOU.

There's nothing wrong with you speaking your truth and sharing your voice when you're coming from a place of respect and love for yourself and others. Speaking your truth doesn't intentionally harm others, and when it's sourced from your innate goodness, it's a form of cultivating healing, peace, and joy within yourself.

A revolution grows when one person speaks up and shares their perspective, which activates truth in another person. The light grows and love spreads.

The underlying desire isn't to create division or amplify old stories of right and wrong. You want to clear the fog and fracture the myths that keep us isolated and separate from each other. Yes, you and your visionary voice have this power. If you trust yourself and wield this energy with care and integrity, there is no limit to how much goodness you can spread.

MAKE ROOM FOR NOT-KNOWING

You know the world is roiling with uncertainty at all times. You can feel it in your bones most days. Change is the only constant in life and it's easy to stay focused on the fear that the ground beneath your feet is on the verge of disintegrating.

Growing up in California, preparing for an inevitable earthquake was part of our back to school routine. We had to bring not just crayons and extra clothes to school, but fresh water, granola bars, and emergency blankets in case the ground ruptured during math class.

A sense of impending chaos was woven deep within my consciousness from the earliest age, not just by earthquake preparedness, but also from the big and little traumas of life at home. I can imagine you have your own memories of an early awareness of instability that are unique to your lived experience.

In whatever ways you learned it wasn't safe to trust the world or the people in your life, those feelings now echo in your present reality as you do the work of listening to yourself and awakening your truth and wisdom.

The work of building self-trust isn't for the faint of heart, and at least from what I can tell, it's a lifelong commitment. My belief is that we have to choose self-trust every day. And we must give ourselves the gift of trust, whether or not we think we deserve it.

Great philosophers, poets, and scholars have long waxed poetic about the truth of life's uncertainty. As the beloved Buddhist teacher Pema Chödrön puts it, what serves us most is "an open state of mind that can relax with paradox and ambiguity."

To reclaim the full power of your visionary voice, you must trust, or at least accept, the wild unknown.

You must welcome the void and relish its open-ended nature of possibility and imagination.

Because your visionary voice isn't here to regurgitate what you've heard or been told. You're here to see what unexpected magic is ready to bubble up to the surface.

> *What if, instead of doubting yourself, you made room to be surprised and delighted?*

> *What if you released your expectations, stepped into a field of self-trust, and waited to see what is ready to unfurl within you?*

WHY DON'T WE TRUST OURSELVES?

For far too long, sensitive souls and creative hearts have been taught, trained, and lauded for suppressing and denying their inner voices and genuine desires.

Whenever you had the audacity to share your boldest ideas, you may have been met with negative labels and harsh judgments:

You live in a fantasy world
You're delusional
This is just wishful thinking
Your ideas are impractical
You're being too idealistic
This sounds ridiculous
It's impossible

Let that list soak in and notice which of them feels most resonant and poignant for you. Which of these spark a flush of shame or the churning stomach of embarrassment?

These are the words you heard growing up to make sure you wouldn't trust yourself or express your vision. You absorbed these judgments at a time in your development when you'd not yet lost the sparkling and effortless connection to your infinite creative potential.

You were still tethered to the cosmos, your soul was linked to the stars, and your inner source of guidance and divine inspiration flowed through you in a healthy, nourishing river of trust.

Fortunately, there is one powerful antidote you can work with that can break down this specific flavor of self-doubt.

Who says?

Take that sentence into your writing life, your creative life, and see what cracks open for you. Every time you meet yourself with blocked energy and hear that inner voice saying things like "you can't do that" just ask yourself, "who says?"

Where are you holding back because you're measuring your dreams against practical standards of other people's definition of so-called success?

> Making art full time is wildly impractical – *who says?*
>
> Writing my book won't make me any money – *who says?*
>
> I can't quit my job to pursue a creative life – *who says?*
>
> Nobody needs the wisdom and stories I have to offer – *who says?*

You're suffocating your dreams too soon, depriving them of the oxygen they need to blossom.

So often, dream impulses arise in non-linear and impractical ways. And no, you probably can't yet tell how the puzzle pieces will all fit together.

But those aren't reasons to abandon your vision altogether. They are invitations for you to surrender and trust. To exercise the powerful energy of faith that brings you into closer relationship with your creative soul and aligns you with your highest path.

It would truly feel better to be rooted in your vision and from that place, to help one beautiful soul, than to help hundreds of people from a place of misalignment.

Your visionary work may provide you a pathway to earning an income that radiantly reflects your dreams. But depending on where you are today, that may or may not match what you imagine it to be. It's perfectly fine to be a creative visionary with a day job. It's perfectly legitimate to fund your passions with a traditional career or as a partner, parent, or caregiver.

When you give up attachments to numbers and specific outcomes, you can send a stronger signal into the world and attract the people and opportunities that will serve and support your highest and best self.

If you trust your desires and ideas more than you trust the opinions of other people, you are well on your way to awakening your visionary voice.

Trusting the unknown path

When you're a visionary, holding space for big dreams, you won't be able to immediately see all the steps it will take to manifest the reality of your big vision from where you stand now.

While this can be excruciatingly frustrating, there are secret benefits to the unknown path. The truth is this: you're a visionary in the process of bringing beautiful things to life. In a culture that tells you to map out a solid plan with detailed action steps, doing things differently can feel uncomfortable.

When it comes to your heart's creative dream or your soul's vision, it's impossible to create a perfectly laid out roadmap ahead of time. Even if this were possible, it's highly impractical and would likely lead you off course or keep you cut off from the beautiful flow of synchronicity and alignment that makes life feel, well, magical.

The problem with waiting for this kind of roadmap is that even if you had one, it might scare you from taking any small steps towards realizing your dreams. It's a bit like saying you want to know the future but then realizing if you had all the answers ahead of time, life wouldn't be as fun anymore. No freedom, no surprise, no fairy dust, no rapture.

What this tension speaks to is that as a visionary, you're amazing at seeing the big picture but sometimes have a hard time figuring out how to make it all happen with the detailed, day-to-day operations.

This dissonance between dream and reality shows up everywhere once you name it with clarity. I can think of at least ten examples right now from my own life, and I imagine you have several that are right there, on the tip of your tongue.

Some of my dreams include building a retreat center in the woods, traveling internationally to lead writing retreats, and becoming a virtuoso frame drummer.

As I write these words, I'm raising two children, building a business, and don't have the energy, time, or commitment level to fully realize any of these dreams right now, let alone in the next 6 to 12 months.

I fully accept this disconnect between my dreams and my reality. I have a feeling of peace and patience because I trust that if these visions are meant to happen, they will unfold perfectly at exactly the right time.

On a deep level, I know that any of my present circumstances can and will change when the time is just right for me to step into this next evolution of my growth. Dreams need time to gestate; rushing them rarely works.

As you let this idea roll around in your mind a bit, what we're moving towards is learning to be self-aware of the energetic essence of our visions. It's a key skill as a visionary to hold an image in your mind that might feel specific or detailed, but to know the reality may differ from this image, even though the essential energy is derived from the same source.

Going back to my examples, the energetic essence of each dream is available to me right now. Writing about what it could look like generates a kaleidoscope of inspiration, ideas, and clarity.

You can also explore and dance with the elements of your big dreams in tangible, doable ways. If you dream of leading retreats, you can start with small local workshops as both an attendee and a leader. You can visit retreat centers to gather inspiration and ideas for how you'd create your own event.

I think the biggest mistake is ignoring the vision and trying to push it out of your mind. It's like rejecting a gift, or saying no to an invitation that was meant just for you.

Don't shut down your big ideas because you can't figure out exactly how it will all fall into place. Befriend your visions, ask them to tell you more, to answer your questions, to reveal more details to you. These prompts help tap into the energetic essence of your dreams, ideas, and visions through your writing:

- *If your vision came to life, how would you feel?*

- *What's the essence of who you'd be and the roles you'd be expressing?*

- *What real world actions and responsibilities would you be performing?*

- *What energetic qualities would you be embodying in this future version of yourself?*

Now look at your current life and recent accomplishments through this lens of awareness.

- *What are you already doing or have already done that carries the energetic essence of your big dreams?*

Write this down and allow yourself to let the truth sink in: you're already on your way to bringing your vision to life.

The key takeaway in this exercise is that you really are dreaming in a way that's rooted in your experience and your skills. You either have or can begin developing the experiences and capabilities you'll need to bring your vision to life in a tangible form that you can feel, see, touch, hear, and enjoy.

HONORING THE INNER VOICE

Your inner voice is always asking you to fulfill your purpose and align with joy. Your essence is here to be shared and to flow out into the world. You're here to add your voice and your truth to the chorus of big-hearted humans circling the planet together in this fleeting moment of aliveness you've chosen together.

You are shaking yourself free from all the spoken and unspoken ways you were taught to doubt yourself along the way. The most powerful thing you can do for your visionary journey is to trust the voice of your inner wisdom, deep knowing, and creative inspiration.

Why? Because when you do, you blossom. You'll do things you never imagined, but it will feel good, like you're finally alive and experiencing life with all your senses. Life unfolds as a series of surprises and synchronicities showing up that are even better than you'd imagined.

Your innate power as a creative being is beyond what you're experiencing right now. You, me, and the great collective of voices rising up into our expanded creative power have only scratched the surface of what's possible when we choose to trust ourselves as a way of being and moving through the world.

Here is my vision: a wave of kindred spirits who consciously reclaim their power, inner radiance, and sacred truth so we can rise together and bring love and light out into the open, to envelop the world with an ocean of energetic healing.

It begins within each of us to make powerful, open-hearted choices for ourselves, our families, and our communities.

The first step is a choice you make to trust yourself. To trust your intuition and follow it, even if it sends out ripples of change in your life and your relationships. Even when others think you're changing, or when your father, sister, or best friend gives you a big, juicy eye roll when you share your insights.

Trust grows with practice. The more you follow through on your intuitive guidance and see how it works in real life, the more you'll learn to speak your own inner language. Like any relationship, the more you communicate, the deeper your ability to trust each other grows.

This is the trust we're after, the trust in our connection to our spiritual, higher selves. When this connection is open, healthy, and flowing with vitality, you can pick apart the difference between a true, sacred YES and a deeply aligned NO to whatever opportunity or choice presents itself on your path.

Through practice, you'll know how to navigate your life with greater confidence and ease. Your ability to discern the sacred yes and no of your inner voice of wisdom will grow more sensitive. You make these choices with greater speed, a deeper level of conviction, and a lightness in your heart as you expand your capacity to accept the support of the divine in your life.

Trusting yourself and stepping up as the leader of your own life is a radical choice. It asks you to take a leap of faith and surrender much of what you were taught growing up about safety and security.

Blind trust leads to self-doubt. It's exactly this kind of doubt that will obscure your visionary voice and keep you separated from yourself. We are told to trust anything and everything except ourselves. To trust our parents, to put blind faith in antiquated social structures, to rely on the security net of a narrow range of possibilities in our work, relationships, and life choices.

Everything on this path of creativity, writing, and claiming your visionary power will come back to trust. It is the fertile soil that allows all your ideas, your truth, and your self-expression to flourish.

Honoring your inner voice requires commitment. In all things, creative and otherwise, you acknowledge yourself as the ultimate authority and the core source of strength in your life.

The word trust is strong, reliable, and steady. It is a firm and solid footing that allows you to build something beautiful and lasting.

Sadly, most of us have learned to find a sense of trust, authority, and strength in the ephemeral realm of 'out there.' We give our trust to others, and consciously or subconsciously, surrender or diminish our creative fire for most of our lives.

Yet trust isn't a onetime switch that gets flipped to the 'on' position. You know this from your relationships with the people in your life. Trust is a wild and alive thing. It can grow and change before your very eyes.

One day you can trust someone completely, and the next day you can discover a betrayal, and see that your trust has crumbled. And likewise, you may have doubts about someone, only to find that over time, they act with so much integrity that you come to trust them with your whole heart.

The most vital relationship to focus on is the one you forge with your self. Before any of the other portals to the visionary realm can be truly unlocked, you must have a basic sense of self-trust that will carry you through your journey of exploration, discovery, and creativity.

Your writing and work in the world can only blossom as much as you're willing to trust yourself to guide your own adventure.

Writing Invitations to Awaken Trust

How does it feel to trust yourself?

When do you feel you cannot be trusted?

Who has told you it's dangerous or unwise to trust your own instincts?

If you trusted yourself completely and fully, what would your life look like?

What choices would you make today from this place of self-trust?

How can you embrace uncertainty in your life?

How can you make room for the dance of delight and surprise?

FREEDOM

Freedom is a wide open landscape for each of us to define, experience, and create. It's a workhorse of a word, too often tossed around with carelessness. It's delicate and fragile while also being powerful and fierce.

If you crack open the word, it reveals this power. Freedom is the right to act, speak, or think as you wish, without being restrained, hindered, or stopped.

And yet, is there such a thing as true freedom? Aren't we always restrained by one thing or another? Our social contracts and the laws of physics all restrict us in some way. Despite the new age mantras of 'believe in miracles' and 'you can have anything you imagine', a deeper part of us knows that life has inherent limits.

These tensions and paradoxes are precisely why you must define freedom for yourself, and get clear on what it means. Otherwise, you may end up chasing a false sense of freedom that will always disappoint you.

Through a Buddhist lens, you could say that freedom is found within the cage, within the boundaries of these limitations and rules. As writers and visionaries, we can access a universe of freedom within our minds and on the page.

It's this limitless source of inner creative freedom that I invite you to cultivate in awakening your visionary voice. When you're glowing with inner freedom, you open a channel to receive inspiration that guides you to share yourself with the world in the way you long to.

Unravel your social conditioning

One of our greatest challenges as creatives, writers, and sensitive souls is that our expansive nature was perceived as threatening or impractical to the people around us. Whether intentionally or not, our families of origin, teachers, and culture all tried to stamp our creativity and wildness out of existence.

Because the messages of limitation and scarcity are so persistent, you probably took on this voice yourself. Depending on where and how you were raised, this internal voice will express itself in unique ways.

From one point of view, I see myself as an educated, privileged, white woman from California. When I shift ever so slightly to the left, I can also see myself as someone who experienced emotional trauma and lives with generalized anxiety disorder. Out of this soil, my internalized voice grew into a thorny vine of misogyny, patriarchy, white supremacy, perfectionism, and submission. This is by no means a comprehensive list, but these are the key elements I've discerned from years of self-awareness, education, and inner listening.

The scripts of this inner voice say things like:

> *You're too much*
>
> *You shouldn't want that*
>
> *Stop being so greedy*

Understanding the source of these critical inner voices is vital for awakening your visionary voice. And I am not suggesting you silence this part of yourself or try to ignore it. I ascribe to the Internal Family Systems belief that these voices played a vital role in our upbringing.

The voice that attempts to keep you quiet believes itself to be serving some noble purpose. Usually it's to keep you safe and maintain your place in whatever social fabric you were born into. As humans, we know how vital a sense of belonging is. We know that if we are dismissed and cast out from our community, our chances of survival plummet.

Freedom isn't achieved by ignoring your social conditioning and silencing the voice within you that values safety over truth-telling. The goal is integration, not further splintering within yourself.

What you can do on the page is listen to this part of you who resists telling the truth. Your creative freedom comes from keeping this channel open and developing compassionate strategies for recognizing and disarming this protector who desires approval over self-expression.

What does creative freedom mean to you?

How do you know when you are not free to express yourself?

Who told you it is not okay or allowed to raise your voice freely?

FREEDOM ON THE PAGE

When you pick up your pen to write what's on your heart and mind, you're exercising your freedom and sovereignty. When you dare to speak the truth in a conversation, you're embodying your right to self-expression.

One opposing force of freedom is censorship. You might be surprised by how pervasive your self-censorship is, whether you're in a group or by yourself. Even when it's just you and a piece of paper, you'll encounter thoughts that tell you it's not safe to say what's really true for you.

If you probe this fear, it usually sounds like a fear of being found out. You feel unsafe to speak your mind, afraid there may be grave consequences for stepping out of line. If you write down what you really think and feel, someone will find this piece of paper and come after you to make you pay a steep price for your defiant transgression.

Early in your life, taking on this dismissive and humiliating internal voice was an effective strategy to stay safe and go unnoticed. You knew how vital it was to belong and be cared for as a small, vulnerable human. Over time, your voice and sense of self shrank until it could fit in a tiny, socially acceptable box, custom built for you.

If you're lucky, this box is still spacious enough to feed your creative heart. You have healthy outlets for your desires and dreams. Yet some of us build an overly tight container for ourselves, with only the faintest traces of light or oxygen passing through.

In this case, your view of what's possible or acceptable becomes so constricted that only a mere pinhole of light remains. The only ideas that can squeeze through this narrow opening have little chance of being planted, let alone nourished, in your life.

Writing is a powerful method for breaking down this box and letting the light back in. You can dismantle these inner walls that were built for your own safekeeping and create a comforting home for yourself.

For many of us creative hearts, the writing we did in our childhood or teen years is precisely what prevented the walls from closing in completely. In my own life, I think books and journals saved me. Being largely ignored in the afternoons when I came home from school, I spent hours with my journals and colored pencils, making words and images. I was also allowed to choose just about any book at the used bookstore, and romanticized the confessional journals of Anaïs Nin.

This freedom to be left alone and read what I pleased is one of the blessings I appreciate from an otherwise stressful time. Anaïs showed me I could say anything I wanted in my journal. I would tell the full and unvarnished truth to myself, even if I was terrified to speak those words out loud to my friends or family.

Writing for yourself, not to please someone else or to receive validation and accolades, is a form of freedom. When you give yourself permission to write in a freewheeling and uncensored way, you can get down to the core of who you are, what you believe, and what you're here to share.

The invitation is this: cultivate freedom in your writing and in your life. Let the writing be a source of freedom, to be a practice of giving yourself permission to be fully and unapologetically your full self.

Give in to your desire to rage, whine, dream, and fantasize on the page. Go all the way with your words. The point is to go big in this safe place and find your limits. Where are your edges? How fierce and wild can you be?

How would it feel to be completely...

> *Unbridled*
> *Untamed*
> *Unlimited*

Freedom is a way to reject the constraints that family, social conditioning, and all the 'isms' place on us from such an early age.

Writing to touch your inner source of freedom unlocks a rich cache of energy, power, and inspiration that usually stays hidden and out of sight.

I also suggest you try going way too far when you're writing. And believe me, I know how powerful the inner censor is. When I'm writing I encounter horrible, embarrassing thoughts that rattle me or stir up shame and guilt. They seem too terrible to admit, let alone write down with my pen onto those creamy pages. At times, I wonder where these thoughts come from or if they even belong to me.

My inner dialogue wonders who will see what I wrote and how harshly will they judge me? I recognize in this moment how much fear I hold in my body. I feel how I carry it with me, always.

And yet, there is an opportunity at that same moment to write these thoughts down as a way of purging and dissolving them. You have the freedom to write it down and then burn the pages and let that stuff go.

They are just words on a page. They can mean everything or they can mean nothing. You have the freedom to choose what you carry and what you let go.

You have the freedom to write one thousand pages of junk until you reach the layer underneath all of that where the gems and diamonds are sparkling with potent prose and visionary ideas.

CLAIM YOUR TRUE NORTH

If you've felt the pull towards something shimmering in the distance, you've experienced the magnetism of your true north. This sense of directional purpose is healthy and well in our childhood, but just like so many of our inborn strengths, it erodes as we walk the path of cultural indoctrination.

Your true north is a guiding presence that always points in the direction of your highest good and your greatest sense of freedom. Reclaiming this inner territory is vital for your visionary awakening.

Each of us has to find our own way to reclaim this north star. It may require you to exert yourself physically until you're too tired to resist it. Or perhaps a flash of awareness will greet you during a silent winter's walk through the snow. Maybe as you're just waking up, you'll experience a calm, quiet presence and awareness that seems to hum with joy.

Claiming true north is a process of listening to your inner voice and prioritizing it over the opinions of anyone else. Perhaps the most important thing to know about this true north is that sometimes it will feel like it's pointing you in the wrong direction.

You'll have to embrace the mystery of your guidance system, and trust that any detours are intentional and connected to some unknown wisdom. A kind of tenacity is required, not just to access your true north, but to follow its lead and see where it hopes to take you.

This requires you to dance all the way to your edges and even push past them slightly. It may feel uncomfortable or unfamiliar, but it also grows your capacity for truthful self-expression. You'll know for yourself how far you can go. Best of all, you'll become present to the bright source of freedom that exists within you.

Writing Invitations
to Awaken Freedom

What is your earliest association with the idea of freedom?

How do you relate to the idea of freedom at this moment?

When did you start to feel that your freedom was restricted or unacceptable?

Where in your home or in the world do you feel most connected to freedom?

What do you need more of to fuel your creative freedom?

PLEASURE

When we allow ourselves to prioritize our need for pleasure and welcome in the energy of our desire, everything in our lives can stitch itself together into a healthy tapestry of creative joy. Infused with pleasure, your creative channel can open, expand, and blossom in its capacity to call through a healthy stream of inspiration, healing, and guidance.

Through pleasure, we tap into a natural state of ease that's so essential for seeing unconventional solutions and pathways to navigate life's blessings and challenges. Too often we overlook the value of pleasure because we have plastered over it with a stifling ethos of work and worthiness.

Do you think of pleasure as a luxury? Is it something you have to withhold or delay until you get all your work done? In Western culture, the echo of puritanical morality continues to teach us that pleasure is suspicious. If it must be acknowledged at all, it's only as a reward for a life of good and pious deeds.

Perhaps the thinking goes that if we prioritized pleasure in our lives, surely we would all abandon our work, ignore our family responsibilities, and stop paying our bills. Yet when you withhold pleasure from yourself, it doesn't ultimately motivate you to make better choices, be more productive, or more connected in our relationships.

Denying ourselves pleasure saps our life force and turns everything we touch into a struggle. It's like oiling your rusty bicycle with sand: everything grinds to a big, messy, gritty halt.

Humans wither and wilt when our creative cauldrons are missing the key ingredient of pleasure. Our ideas keep falling flat and we lose touch with our clarity, vision, focus, and purpose.

We must feed ourselves regularly with pleasure, to see it and surround ourselves with it in order to nurture our visionary voice. There are countless creative gifts that arise from making pleasure a priority in our daily habits and routines.

The biggest point of confusion I notice is that pleasure gets conflated with hedonism or narcissism. If you notice you believe pleasure is something you can only enjoy at the expense of someone else in your life, you're likely caught up in a tangled belief system that needs to be gently dissolved.

Experiencing pleasure in ways that are both big and small helps you come alive. And when you are at your most alive, you can love other people, support them, and connect with them in deeper, healthier ways. Each of us needs pleasure as a form of sweetness in life that brings us to a natural state of balance and creative vitality.

PLEASURE AS CREATIVE ALCHEMY

We all want to experience the thrill of taking raw materials, sticks, mud, and dreams, and turning them into something new and unique. For you, it may be dancing, writing, painting, building, knitting, or gardening. Preparing beautiful food, making music, or adorning your body with jewels and ink could all feed your creative desires.

The common thread is a desire to shape your environment and a pleasure we experience from making our mark on the world around us. At the root of these desires is the uniquely human need to declare to ourselves and the world that we are here. We are alive and we have a voice. We want to proclaim with joyous, glee-filled confidence that we exist and have a gift to offer the world and the sacred circle of human life.

I believe in simple, everyday pleasures as the primary source of fuel to enliven all of your senses and feel grounded in your true creativity. By noticing and appreciating these commonplace moments of pleasure, you can also fill your writing and creative work with rich, sensory details that resonate with others because they are so alive with feeling and the soul of life.

Pleasure is received by our senses and alchemized by our minds. We have the ability to translate sound, touch, taste, beauty, and movement into an entire world of meaning. Sitting still by a babbling brook, you might notice that the steady murmuring soothes your nervous system. Maybe it reminds you that movement is healthy, and everything is following its own path of destiny.

Early in the morning, you're the first to wake up and the house is silent. You brew your favorite coffee and pour it into that one mug you picked out from a local pottery shop. You settle into your favorite chair by the window and watch the sky change from gray, to pink, to orange, while the sun rises over the trees. Everything lights you up - the smell of the coffee, the feeling of that smooth mug in your hand, and the dazzling sight of the sky before your eyes.

This is a moment of supreme pleasure, presence, and joy. It's rich with details, sensations, and beauty. It fills you up deeply and you notice how much more present and embodied you feel by taking time to sit with yourself in this state of quiet observation.

Creative alchemy is the process of taking the tiniest details in life and turning them into something that soothes, inspires, or uplifts us. The world is always offering us reminders that there is pleasure just in the very fact of being alive. When we let this into our awareness, it fuels our ability to see the truth, name it with clarity, and unleash our visionary voice.

Expressing ourselves in a tangible way, such as gardening, knitting, and cooking, allows us to enter a state of flow from being so incredibly present with the task at hand. Moving a pen across the page, letting a string of words form on the paper, gives us this same physical experience.

Most of us love the inner spaciousness this sort of concentration and work cultivates within us. We're transported and transfixed. We relish the unique pleasure in doing something with our own two hands, and time expands while we're immersed in a physically creative process.

It's also immensely satisfying and life affirming to have a finished product as a tangible reward for our dedicated effort. Just as a young child in kindergarten is delighted at the prospect of his turn at show and tell, we share this desire to bring things to life and share them with people we love.

To nourish your own well of creative alchemy, reflect on these questions:

> *What moments in your day are already a source of pleasure?*

Do you need to slow down to notice the pleasure that already exists in your life?

What are your favorite ways of working with your hands in your daily life?

How are those passions or hobbies connected to your visionary voice?

Are there moments of pleasure in your life you're too busy to notice?

How can you give yourself room to experience even more pleasure on a daily basis?

PRODUCTIVITY VERSUS PLEASURE

What often blocks us from experiencing more pleasure is over-valuing productivity. Taking this further, we believe that productivity requires work, effort, sacrifice, struggle, and possibly even suffering.

Especially if you identify as a recovering perfectionist, this tension is likely to be well and alive in your creative life. Even if you start with the intention of letting your writing take you where it wants to go, at some point you wonder if you're just wasting your time.

This only leads to even more constriction and blocked creativity. Your visionary ideas get shut down before they even have a chance to show you what possibilities might want to emerge in your life.

Writing can be an absolutely perfect way to untangle these mixed up ideas about what is and is not 'worth' your time and energy. Rather than putting pressure on yourself for your visionary voice to give you productive ideas, try approaching your self-expression with a spirit of curiosity.

> *Can you enjoy the process of giving yourself time to think and dream?*

> *Can you give yourself permission to write and create without an agenda, or without proof that it was 'worthy' of someone else's measuring stick?*

You can flip this entire concept around and look at it with fresh eyes. What if the act of choosing pleasure and making time to nourish your creative spirit is exactly what you need to be more nourished and ultimately, more "productive" in the long run?

Another way to turn this around is to question what you believe about productivity. Whose definition of productivity are you carrying? Is productivity linked in your mind to how much money you make or how many people praise you for your hard work and results?

There is nothing inherently wrong with desiring accomplishment, validation, and appreciation. But if you're denying yourself pleasure and ignoring your visionary voice because you think it's a waste of time, part of you is on a track for some form of burnout.

It's time to separate creativity from productivity so you can appreciate and celebrate the energy of intention, process, and vision. Just imagine that honoring your innate love of pleasure is a way of creating true vitality and sustainable wellbeing.

What do you need to believe for yourself to make pleasure a priority in your life, creatively and otherwise?

Is pleasure selfish?

Pleasure also gets a bad reputation for being a source of selfishness. But this couldn't be further from the truth. Making pleasure a priority is vital for your emotional, mental, physical, and spiritual health. It is a fundamental human right to enjoy the life you are living.

Whether or not it's conscious, if you deny yourself pleasure in favor of more work and more productivity, you end up with a deficit in your pleasure reserves. Pleasure for us is like sunlight and water for plants - without it, we droop, fade, and get crunchy.

Your creative soul suffers from this drought. Maybe your thinking gets foggy, which makes you irritable and grumpy. Every day you're just a little more listless or bored. Your writing feels monotonous, and there's just no juice when you sit down with your pen and paper.

Right now, today, I invite you to say this with me: pleasure is NOT selfish.

Pleasure is fuel, food, and nourishment. In all forms and facets, allowing yourself to fully experience and receive pleasure revives your senses and restores your energy. It brings you back into the flow of aliveness and joy.

The only validity to saying "pleasure is selfish" is when thinking of the habit of seeking shadow pleasures when our life has gotten a bit flat. If you're starting from a place of lack and deprivation, when the opportunity presents itself to have a taste of pleasure, you might over-indulge in unhealthy substitutes for the deeper experience of pleasure you're truly seeking.

When I'm rushing around in constant work and productivity mode, I end up feeling deeply drained and depleted. I keep making withdrawals from my pleasure account until it's at a zero or even a negative balance. Craving relief and a surge of energy to refill my empty pleasure tank, I might turn to an accessible indulgence that mimics the experience of a deeper and more lasting source of pleasure. These are temporary mood-boosters, like chocolate and wine, or shopping for another pair of gold hoop earrings.

These stand-ins might give a jolt of energy, but ultimately they leave me saddled with more stuff and only a fleeting experience of pleasure. There is no lasting contentment, and if I'd just allowed myself to do something more deeply nourishing, I would feel so much more rejuvenated.

If you're resonating with this picture, I invite you to take a deep breath of compassion and love, and know that you're not alone in this experience. Also, this pattern doesn't mean there's anything wrong with you. Instead, what we're uncovering is the broken system and context in which we're living and the sad truth that we've been separated from our essential self that knows what an authentic experience of pleasure feels like.

What might happen with your creative practice if you allowed yourself to choose pleasure over obligation or productivity?

Is the very act of writing a source of pleasure in your life? Perfect, then you get to tell your friends and family that your creative time is vital for your health. You literally need that writing time to keep yourself well.

Healthy sources of pleasure come to us in the form of intimate connections with friends and family or the pleasure of being seen for our true selves in a safe and positive way by our community. There is pleasure in channeling our life force energy into creating things that are truly valuable and appreciated by other people.

And isn't that far from selfish?

FINDING YOUR PATH TO PLEASURE

There are 1,000 doorways that lead to pleasure, and your only job is to find the ones that work best for you. One tension that comes up for writers is that our work can keep us very much stuck in our heads. This is why the following suggestions are visceral and centered on the body.

My hope is that these ideas get your juices flowing and you notice what lights you up and gets you excited. Ideally, you'll find ways to make space for pleasure in your daily routines and rhythms, so that pleasure is inextricably woven into your life. It's not an afterthought or something that's haphazardly stuck on to other things. It's just a natural part of how you move through the world, and it brings contentment, love, and connection to all parts of your life.

Movement

Dancing, walking, swimming, and most forms of physical activity help you enter a state of presence and pleasure. Bodies are all different, and these movements could be big or small, dramatic or subtle.

However you feel inspired to do so, your body comes alive through movement. Maybe it's a neck roll and some gentle yoga. If you have more energy, it could be a cathartic dance session with lots of hip circles and wild hair.

No matter how you move, the intention is to let your energy circulate and flow. Let your awareness of what feels good come back online. Take your movement practice a step further by stopping to really notice what your body is asking for next.

Does it want to loosen up and be less rigid? Maybe it wants to slow down, or perhaps to speed up. We are fortunate to have so many sources of movement inspiration at our fingertips in this modern world.

Movement literally changes your brain chemistry and releases feel-good hormones, like dopamine and serotonin, into your bloodstream. It supports you in letting go of toxins, relieving stress, and leaves behind calm, happiness, and peace.

Try moving before you write, and also experiment with moving after you write. How does your sense of clarity or self-expression shift when you allow your body to move the way it wants to?

Nourishment and hydration

This might sound silly, but anecdotal evidence suggests that nearly 75% of adults in the United States are chronically dehydrated. For most of us, this is caused by a combination of factors, like drinking caffeine, spending time in climate controlled environments, and simply forgetting to take the time to drink water throughout the day.

I am guilty of all of these. I recently had to dial back my coffee habit from four cups a day to just one cup a day because of how much it was interfering with my adrenal system. When I replaced all that coffee with water and herbal tea, the change was almost immediate. My sleep, memory, and writing all improved after just a few weeks.

When we are hydrated, everything feels better, which is how I see this being connected to pleasure and creativity.

The same goes for our food. Many of us rush through meals and perhaps we don't even remember what our food tasted like after it's done. What if you slowed down and enjoyed the experience of nourishing yourself with each meal and savoring every bite?

These practices aren't meant to activate a wave of guilt or overthinking. This is only an invitation to slow down and notice what you're taking in. To enjoy the experience of sipping your sparkling water in a beautiful, chilled glass. Or arranging a rainbow of sliced fruit for yourself and really noticing the taste, texture, and sweetness of each piece.

We need food to thrive, and gifting yourself with the time and space to savor this experience reconnects with the truth of your innate worthiness.

TIME IN NATURE

The natural world is a spectacle of pleasure. Simply standing outside, with eyes open or closed, and breathing into the space of the world around you, connects you with the nourishment of the earth. We crave the pleasure of connecting to the ultimate source of life, Gaia, our mother earth.

We live in a time where nature deficit disorder is a real thing for adults and children alike. Depending on where you live and work, it could feel out of reach to spend more time in nature. Yet even in the most urban environments, wild plants and animals find ways to exist and push through the concrete landscape.

If you need small, regular doses of nature, you can get your fill just by walking outside, taking in the blue of the sky, or standing in a sunny spot to feel the warmth and radiance of the sun.

For a longer adventure with nature, you could try one of the many nature-based therapy activities that have emerged in recent years. Some of my favorite ways to commune with the renewing energy of the earth include:

> **Forest bathing** - sit quietly in a natural spot and practice mindfulness of the sights, sounds, and sensations around you with your eyes and heart open.

Tree whispering – place your hands on a tree and engage in a reciprocal dialogue of sharing what's on your heart, and opening to receive any messages from the world of living things.

Earthing and grounding – stand with bare feet on the grass or lay directly on the ground to come into a deeper contact with the earth.

Herbalism and foraging – go on a plant walk to notice what's growing along the edges of a trail or the weedy patches of a park. *(Please note I don't recommend ingesting anything without the guidance of an expert in plant identification!)*

Wild swimming – a watery plunge in natural places, like rivers, ponds, lakes, and the ocean that is enlivening, healing, and strengthening.

However you choose to engage with nature as a restorative practice can offer you immediate benefits in body, mind, and spirit. You might experience the pleasure of gaining a fresh perspective or wider viewpoint on how things work, or what is truly important to you.

These interactions with the natural world also reconnect you with the natural cycles of creativity, from the seed of an idea to the nurturing of a dream until it reaches the peak of fruition.

Rest

Sometimes what your wild animal body craves is simply to rest. Whether it's getting to bed early or taking time in the afternoon to sit down with a cup of tea and do absolutely nothing else, when do you allow yourself to deeply rest and relax?

When I was drinking my four cups of coffee a day, I didn't even notice my sleep signals in the evening. Once I dialed back all that caffeine, I was surprisingly exhausted by 8pm every night. I had been overriding those basic urges and slowly depleting all of my rest reserves year after year.

In your own life, where have you been overriding the urge to rest, and how can you honor those natural calls to slow down and make time for relaxation?

Writing Invitations
to Awaken Pleasure

What does your body long for in order to experience more pleasure?

Where have you chosen productivity over pleasure recently?

Which pleasure practices do you feel inspired to weave into your creative practice?

How does it feel to write about pleasure?

Where do you feel resistance to experiencing more pleasure?

How are you defining pleasure for yourself?

CLARITY

When you say you want clarity, what are you really asking for? To be assured that you won't make a mistake? Or to perfectly understand what your visionary voice is suggesting you do or create in your life?

Yearning for clarity is another way of expressing your desire to know and understand what you are really here to do or bring into the world. But waiting for clarity before you try something new will keep you stuck in an infinite loop of self-doubt and procrastination.

Demanding a steady state of clarity is really just a way to fight with reality. The journey of a visionary is a twisting road that zigs and zags. Most of the time, you can scarcely see a few hundred yards ahead, let alone the entire path to your desired destination. But if you trust yourself to keep moving forward, appreciate the thrill of navigating all the hairpin turns, and marvel at the grandeur of your surroundings, you can enjoy the ride.

If you're waiting and wishing for your visionary awakening to follow the route of a flat, predictable speedway cutting through an urban wasteland, you'll be sorely disappointed.

What I'm really saying is that clarity isn't static, it isn't a destination that offers the right answer, at the right time, every time. Clarity is more like the Moon, following a natural and somewhat predictable cycle between brilliance and elusiveness and back again. It requires the visionary soul to enjoy the darkness and moments of doubt with an open heart and a courageous, faithful spirit. And if you're up for the challenge, this will make the flashes of clarity even more dazzling and inspiring.

CLARITY IS A NATURAL CYCLE

I love using the lunar cycle to understand how clarity expresses itself in your creative life. Just like the Moon, clarity plays a game of hide and seek in spirals and circles. One day the Moon is full and you feel a sense of absolute clarity. You can see everything in perfect detail, and the gestalt of your vision feels as real as the back of your own hands.

Then you set out to write what you saw and capture it in a way that makes it tangible. But the more you work or write, the more you seem to lose what you just grasped. Over time, you feel that your clarity has slipped away and become lost.

Where did clarity go? Why has it abandoned us? Just when you're completely disoriented and doubt if you ever had clarity to begin with, another glimmer of light returns and you notice a familiar flicker out of the corner of your eye.

You retrace the path you'd been walking and pick back up where you left off, determined to leave a few more clues behind to help you through the darkness the next time it descends.

This pattern of clarity found and clarity lost is a natural, predictable unfolding. If you choose to embrace it, you can harvest the gifts it has to offer.

As much as we think we want clarity, what you might really be grasping for is certainty. Is it possible that your definition of clarity is just certainty and perfectionism dressed up for a costume party? Perhaps your pursuit of clarity is linked to a swirl of murky concerns about making mistakes, messing things up, or failing at something you care about.

When you notice thoughts like "If I had clarity, I wouldn't slip up or waste my time," or "If I had clarity, I'd know exactly where I was going and could get there faster," then you can be sure that perfectionism, and therefore fear, has grasped the reins.

Let's return to that image of a gentle cycle, where clarity is like breathing. It comes and goes easily and naturally, in and out, up and down. Clarity is the state of being clear, to be in a state where things are luminous, free from doubt, and serene. From that perspective, we can embrace clarity as a state of awareness and a willingness to see what exists before us.

While we can learn from the lightness of clarity, we can also expand our wisdom and awareness in its absence. Being separated from clarity from time to time provides an opening, when the field is dark and unknown, to see opportunities and connections that weren't available when your gaze was fixed on a single point of certainty.

These are the moments when surprise and delight can slip in and present you with gifts that make your heart leap up with joy and pleasure. This is the time when your field can lay fallow, providing space for the deep, unseen work of integration and synthesis.

This expression of clarity can coexist with a feeling of surrender and trust. We can embrace this state of being blissfully directionless while still holding tight to our sense of self and purpose.

A visionary life does not follow a straight line. Let's help each other remember this, deep in our bones, and welcome the ease and relief it brings. Your creative process doesn't need to adhere to a linear structure.

You can spiral your way to greatness. You can walk in circles and still make progress. Just like climbing a mountain, when the goal is evolution, enlightenment, and reaching the pinnacle of your soul's purpose, a circling path is the most enjoyable and graceful way to rise to the peak.

SEEING BELOW THE SURFACE

To the visionary voice within you, clarity is a way to peer beneath the surface of life and gaze at the deeper truth of things. It can be helpful to think of the quality of clarity like keeping your eyes soft and open, allowing a wide range of peripheral vision to come into your awareness.

This is an open, trusting, and vulnerable place to stand. It requires more curiosity and wonder than force, speed, or momentum. To hold clarity like this asks you to relax, trust, and simply observe the world around you. In this patient stillness, the silvery glimpses of clarity can find you and whisper their messages, offering direction and insight.

Writing with clarity in this way, cultivating a state of attentiveness and wonder with the words on the page, fine tunes your ability to see and make sense of the world. I believe that clarity is a practice, not a destination.

Instead of trying to reach a conclusion, what if you approached clarity like a kaleidoscope that could show you new colors and angles to an idea or a situation? Some writing prompts you can work with to cultivate this habit are:

What if I looked at it the other way?

How might this idea be true?

How might this idea not be true?

What would I have said about this five years ago?

How has my view on this already changed?

When I'm trying to make out the shape and nuance of my visionary inspiration, I always see myself by a stream or a pond. There's something potent about the idea of knowing that an entire ecosystem of magic exists below the surface of a body of water that helps me find my source of depth and momentum.

If you want to feel more clear or settled about something, imagine yourself by a body of water. Perhaps you see yourself on the sandy beach of a glassy lake, or on the moss-covered rocks besides a gurgling forest stream. Then ask yourself, 'what lies beneath the surface?'

In the case of a lake, there are so many layers beneath that mirrored surface that first greets you. There are plants and fish making their home there. Layers of rocks and sand and mud. Below them, what else exists? And what are you meant to learn from the ecosystem that frames the pond, the trees, shrubs, birds, animals, and trails surrounding its edges?

You may have a different image that helps you connect with the experience of depth and detail this practice is meant to unlock. Whatever your visionary voice is trying to show you or share with you, ask for more details. Open yourself up to seeing the bigger context and the deeper layers. Look for the texture and nuance in whatever wants to express itself through you and honor these elements. Not by being attached to them, but by listening to what wants to emerge.

Some of what comes through may be quite literal and specific. But more often than not, your visionary voice will use symbols, images, and sensations to give you the feeling of whatever it's inviting you to create, build, or bring into form.

This is the language of archetype your visionary voice knows by heart, and it can take time and practice to translate that into words. Never doubt for a second that you have exactly what you need to make sense of these messages. Keep listening, keep writing, and stay open to the connections and clarity that want to emerge.

LET CLARITY BREATHE

Perhaps the most important truth I've discovered about clarity is that it cannot thrive in your mind, it must exist in your body and in the world. You may think you're completely clear about what you want and what your visionary voice is hoping to create, but if you don't partner those thoughts with real world action, nothing is actually happening.

Clarity comes from action and communicates with us through all our senses. It is our embodied knowing, that full body sense of 'yes' or 'no' that gives us the most potent and useful information on our visionary path.

Especially if you have a habit of overthinking things, or spending endless hours making plans without taking real world action, this shift in perspective can dramatically expand your creative process.

As you engage with your visionary ideas through your writing practice, you'll eventually need to test them with actual humans and kindred spirits. It's not enough to let all that goodness languish on the page of your journal. The point is to let your visions breathe and bring them out into the sun.

We'll take my recent love of drums as an example of what this looks like. Over the course of a year, I found myself with a persistent question about how to make my creative practice richer and more embodied. I wasn't sure what that meant or what it was supposed to look like. I just kept feeling the urge to try something different and heard some confusing whispers from my inner voice.

By staying open to this voice and being willing to have no idea what I was supposed to do, eventually the messages crystallized, both in my personal writing sessions and in conversations with friends. As the picture slowly came into focus, I was beyond surprised when I realized my visionary voice wanted me to learn how to play a frame drum.

I was quite curious how frame drumming could be connected to my writing work. But I followed the call and I started watching drumming videos. Then I bought a drum and started to practice. I bought a few more drums and continued teaching myself to play.

Within a few months, I finally put all the pieces together and realized that my drumming practice was another form of expression for my visionary voice. It has also become a powerful healing tool for regulating my sensitive nervous system.

Now I drum before I write to help me settle into myself and to activate a steady connection with my inner voice. Growing this part of my life and my creative practice feels deeply nourishing and restorative, and I hardly remember what life was like before my office was filled with not just journals, but a growing collection of frame drums.

In your own life and creative practice, what kind of action is needed to bring your ideas out into the world so they can reveal themselves to you? Ultimately, this is the lesson here: you can't completely understand many of your visionary ideas until you allow them to grow, dance, and play in the sun and fresh air of real, daily life.

When you commit to expressing your visionary ideas, in even the smallest ways, you can see and feel how they want to unfurl and change. You learn so much about yourself when you test your dreams and ideas in this way, and it also reinforces the truth that you can trust the vision and inspiration you're receiving.

Writing Invitations to Awaken Clarity

For each of the prompts below, write about why that statement is true for you.

Clarity…

> *Is a choice*
>
> *Is felt in the body*
>
> *Doesn't live in the mind*
>
> *Originates in the heart*
>
> *Is a state of being*
>
> *Is a natural expression of the creative cycle*
>
> *Ebbs and flows*
>
> *Broadens my perspective*

COURAGE

In any creative, visionary life you will encounter resistance, both within yourself and from others. Developing a courageous heart that can welcome this resistance and skillfully dissolve it is essential for keeping your creative energy flowing.

Fear and resistance arise, over and over again. They are simply part of the unfurling process of growth, evolution, and creative becoming we sign up for in this human life. What we must remember is that fear and resistance aren't signs you should abandon your visionary ideas, stop writing, or give up on what you care about. Resistance is just another catalyst for cultivating courage and compassion.

There may be a million different ways resistance shows up for you. The reason we're talking about this here is so you can dissolve this resistance more easily and quickly, more of the time. You will need big, heaping doses of this creative courage and skill on your journey of visionary awakening.

We face countless flavors of resistance in our lives, creatively and otherwise. We're afraid of failure, and equally afraid of success. What price will we have to pay for our happiness or our freedom? We have old patterns of lack, scarcity and not enoughness. Not to mention, as humans, we're fundamentally wired to avoid risk and change.

Resistance lives in our minds and also our bodies. I had a profound realization of that truth in a Mirror Walk at a women's circle gathering one lovely Fall Equinox. I was partnered with a stranger I'd never met before, then was blindfolded so she could gently guide me through the wooded terrain.

In this state of voluntary blindness, relying on some-one else for a sense of direction, I was stiff and tense. My whole body was rigid with a fear of falling and I became physically aware of how little I trusted myself without my sense of sight. Honestly, I did not trust this perfect stranger to take care of me in this vulnerable state.

With each stiff, awkward step, I became deeply aware of how this same resistance was present in my daily life, even with my eyes wide open. I decided to experiment with letting go and consciously relaxing my body. I exhaled, dropped my shoulders, and played with what it could feel like to be fluid and soft, yielding and gentle.

I let my body sway and glide with more ease, more grace. As my knees softened and I connected with my heart center, I felt more confident in myself. My awareness dropped out of my head, with its swirl of thoughts, and I brought my energy into my core so I could be present in my whole body. I didn't fall or stumble, because I trusted myself to stay connected to the earth beneath my feet, no matter who was walking beside me.

This is the kind of courage I believe we all need on the visionary path. The courage to trust yourself and stay open to connecting with others. This softening and relaxing gives you more resilience and strength than you can access from a state of rigid resistance.

Courageous dreaming

One place where visionaries shut themselves down is at the very beginning stages of the dreaming process. You might notice a bubble of light wanting to make its way to the surface and you immediately clamp it right back down.

It doesn't feel safe to even consider dreaming a new dream. The idea of discovering something that will ask you to change your entire life is so threatening and scary, you won't even allow yourself to think a new thought for a single second.

Maybe it's not quite this dramatic for you, and it just feels more like you're stuck in your same creative grooves, making things the same way over and over again. It's not bad, but it's not exciting. And you've gotten quite comfortable with this, *thank you very much*, and you don't need to pay attention to your dreams right now.

But what if you're simply afraid to dream because you're afraid your heart will break? Is it possible you're worried that if you allow your visionary voice to wake up and share its dreams, you'll only end up feeling disappointed or foolish?

What if you let your heart dream its big dreams and then you tell someone about them? They might laugh at you for daring to dream so big and they'll swiftly remind you that you are just too much. The whole world will laugh at us for having the audacity to listen to our dreams, and if things don't turn out exactly how we imagined them, everyone will know we failed.

I get it, these are big fears. As an intelligent, tender-hearted, and empathic human being, you probably feel these fears deeply. It's not always easy to get space from these thoughts and concerns that continually hold you back.

This is where courageous dreaming provides a nurturing and healing process that makes space for your visionary voice to shine through. Courageous dreaming is simply the act of giving yourself permission to dream big, without giving energy to the fears and internal pushback that may have become so automatic, you take them for granted.

The alternative I'm offering is to consistently and lovingly allow yourself to enjoy the process of dreaming and visioning for its own sake, without connecting it to success or failure. You can dream and keep it to yourself! You don't need to immediately rush into the world, sharing your lovely ideas with people who are also afraid to tap into their visionary nature.

In fact, one of the things you'll find on the visionary path is a growing need to review your inner circle of kindred spirits, and surround yourself with people who are both grounded and imaginative. When you do feel ready to share your ideas with others, you either need to be deeply anchored in what you're saying so you can shake off any doubts, or be mindful about only trusting your dreams with the people in your life who can listen without judgment or problem-solving.

Think about how these patterns of fear and resistance are showing up in your creative life right now.

> *Do you stop yourself from dreaming before you start?*
>
> *Can you enjoy the process of dreaming and visioning without getting caught up in figuring out how to 'make it work?'*

Who in your life can listen to your ideas without judgment?

Give yourself permission to follow your visionary voice where it wants to lead you. Allow this voice to express itself on the page when you're writing. Listening does not mean you need to take action, at least not right away. This is just a practice of compassionate inner listening, and cultivating the courage to go slow, breathe deeply, and trust yourself.

As you continue listening, you're developing your inner strength and resilience to move through this resistance over and over again. Courageous dreaming is not a practice of silencing your doubts or crushing your resistance. This is a practice of deep self-love that allows your visionary voice to thrive, shine, and blossom.

Nourish your heart

Being a visionary will ask you to say yes to yourself until it feels as natural as waking up each morning. This is brave work, big-hearted work, and you have the courage to answer that call.

Yet you can't let the intensity of this boldness take over. You want to smolder, not burn like wild, and suddenly flame out. This is where your visionary journey requires you to tend to your inner and outer fires to keep yourself in equilibrium.

Have you ever considered it an act of courage and bravery to make sure you're taking exquisite care of yourself? Or, in your mind, is courage reserved for heroic acts of self-sacrifice?

In each of these visionary qualities there is some uncoupling that needs to happen, and in the case of courage, it's that superhero sacrifice that usually must get unstuck. Some days, I think the bravest thing you can do is take such good care of yourself that you live until you are 103.

These courageous acts of self-care aren't likely to be glamorous, they are probably small and simple. Longevity is highly associated with simple things like not being stressed out, maintaining great friendships, and keeping your mind engaged by always learning new things.

Just as being a visionary is your birthright, your courage is one of your innate gifts. Explore this natural courage as you consider what a fully expressed version of you wants to do and experience.

How are you already brave?

What are your everyday acts of self-love?

Can you give yourself more of those moments?

When you have a big cause that you care about, it's easy to let it take over your life. It's easy to get swept away in serving that bigger purpose, but in a way that costs you dearly.

Numerous social and cultural factors play into our fear, hesitancy, and overwhelm, and I know how important it is to acknowledge and validate each of them. Yet this is exactly why choosing joy, choosing to rest, and having the audacity to tend to your creative life is so powerful and revolutionary.

Being brave can happen when you're writing in your journal, it can show up in your books and creative projects. Courage is a state of mind that asks us to cultivate a habit of moving through resistance with an open heart, and making your art anyway.

Fear of the exciting unknown

I'm sure you've heard things like "feel the fear and do it anyway" or "tell your fear to eff-off." To which I respond with a big, heavy sigh. These intense reactions to fear are misinformed at best, and at worst, make it seem like you could do anything you wanted if you just controlled your mind with anger and internal yelling. We cannot sustainably move through resistance by the brute force, self-denial, or internalized punishment we see from so many 'tough-love' advice-givers.

What I'd like to offer you is the idea that there are different flavors of fear. There are many intelligent writers and psychotherapists who have explored this in great detail, but I will courageously dip my toes in these waters anyway because it provides such a helpful framework for self-understanding, courage, and creative growth.

We are born with a healthy, life-preserving fear response. Our minds and bodies are designed to recognize threats and to react to them to keep us safe. This fear response is healthy and wonderful, and it's ultimately responsible for the survival of the whole human race.

But you and I could sit down to write our opinions on a piece of paper, and while we're sipping an oat-milk cappuccino, we imagine someone reading our words, getting furious with us for what we said, and whoops, all of a sudden we've activated our primal fear response.

Now you're sweating a little and a knot in your stomach forms. Absolutely nothing has happened, except clicking some keys on a computer and following up that cappuccino with a freshly baked chocolate croissant. But our bodies may as well be facing down a saber-toothed tiger.

Our minds are so powerful that we can feel nearly the same level of physical fear about an imagined, hypothetical response to our words as if we're in dire, mortal danger. This is the fear we want to learn how to dissolve, because it will hold us back from our creative life and visionary ideas.

One of the most effective ways to tame this fear is by noticing these moments and praising our nervous systems for being so clever and trying so very hard to keep us safe. You can even try talking to your physical fear response like a beloved pet, "I see you're trying to protect me from the opinions of strangers and you think something really terrible will happen if we write that article. Thank you for doing your job, you can go have a cookie, I'm going to get back to writing!"

Our fear response isn't meant to be dismantled. That isn't our goal. But turning that system back into the 'off' position after it's been activated by a hypothetical situation is a skill we must all develop and sustain.

Now we're clear that we have healthy fear for a good reason and that same healthy fear can be misdirected at situations that aren't life-threatening. This brings us to a third flavor of fear that isn't talked about as often: fear of the exciting unknown.

Fear of the exciting unknown can trigger a panic or flight reaction, but there's more to it below the surface. If you slow down and feel into the deeper realm of your fear, you may notice a little excitement. Or an expansiveness, a yearning within you.

We want to pay attention to these deep inner cues, as they are flares that are trying to reach our conscious minds. That flicker of excitement is an energetic breadcrumb, it's the visionary within you saying 'yes, I want this!' Or at least 'this is interesting, this is moving closer to the direction of our big ideas!'

If we tend to our hearts and cultivate our courage, the ability to identify this fear of the exciting unknown can grow stronger and stronger.

What does fear of the exciting unknown look and feel like? It's usually activated by an opportunity that presents itself, or a possibility that surfaces within our minds. Then a response is triggered, such as:

> *I'm scared to speak on stage at this local conference, yet I keep seeing myself with a microphone in hand, delivering an inspiring talk.*

> *I have no idea why I want to write a book since I don't think I'm a great writer, yet I feel strangely excited about it anyway.*

In these cases, you may be experiencing the fear of stepping into uncharted territory, even though you feel excited about it. Rather than pure terror, you might notice that attached to this so-called fear are other emotions like curiosity, wonder, and anticipation.

You're feeling a call to try something different and set foot in uncharted territory. This is a beautiful thing, a crossing of a threshold from one phase of your work into a higher level. You realize some risk is involved, but your visionary voice continues to nudge you forward and things may even feel like they're lining up with surprising ease.

These are all signs that you're answering your calling and creative courage is a potent ally at these times.

Writing Invitations to Awaken Courage

Where do you feel called to step into the exciting unknown?

What do you believe about courage?

How does it feel to be brave in your writing?

How does it feel to be brave with your dreams?

What does your heart need to feel nourished and courageous?

INTUITION

Intuition isn't necessarily the source of your visionary ideas, it's a feedback system to help you discern which way to go and what to pay attention to. By definition, intuition is a way of knowing. Specifically, it's the ability to understand something through a felt or sensed awareness, rather than through conscious reasoning. Fortunately, it's also a skill you can practice and strengthen, and it serves a vital purpose in awakening your visionary voice.

When you look at intuition this way, it becomes practical and grounded. It doesn't need to be a mystical phenomenon that eludes you or remains out of reach. I invite you to consider that you can treat your intuition as a tool that can be tended and kept in good working condition.

Just like any system, all the parts have to work together for the whole to function. When your intuition is healthy and well-nourished, it fuels your creative process. You're able to hear your visionary voice with clarity and take action on your desires and insights.

Through the feedback system of your intuition, you can navigate the physical world with more ease and more self-trust. You will know when you're on the right track, and you'll know when you're veering off course.

INTUITIVE WAYS OF KNOWING

Intuition is another way of saying receptivity. When you develop your intuition, you're expanding your ability to hear and receive messages from an imaginal realm of energetic knowing. Writing is one of the most effective methods I've encountered to strengthen and cultivate this expansive form of whole-hearted perception.

Over time, I've come to believe some basic truths about intuition and the role it has played in a life of creativity and writing.

Intuition is...

- a connection to our higher selves.

- a form of communication that tethers us to the divine.

- the guidance system that helps us to know when we're on the path that's serving our highest and best good.

- a source of feedback to realize when we're veering off our true path.

I find it fascinating that intuition has been treated in our culture as something to be skeptical about. That somehow our ability to sense non-verbal, non-linear, energetic information about the world around us is suspect.

Intuition is wild and unruly, so it's no wonder it's diminished and dismissed in our society. If you look at your intuition as a compass, it becomes a tool that is always trying to lead us to our true North. And few things are more dangerous that independent thinkers with a strong desire to change the system.

Intuition is a form of wisdom that can't be completely explained or understood from a purely rational, scientific perspective. We can't prove or logically explain how we knew we needed to take that trip to Vietnam or withdraw from that PhD program.

All we can say is that it felt right, or we just knew we had to do it. Something inside us made us say yes or no, and even we felt slightly perplexed about the decision we made or how clear it all felt. We're simply following the road signs to help us stay on the path as we make our soul's journey in this lifetime.

When honored and celebrated, our source of intuitive information becomes a sacred tool for making choices and decisions that point us in the direction of our dreams and a visionary life.

If intuition is a source of information, a stream of higher consciousness and wisdom we have access to, then how are we receiving and translating these messages? What is the mechanism for recognizing our intuition?

The most potent tool for receiving intuitive wisdom and information is our body, and often in particular, our heart. What our body is typically picking up and then communicating to our mind is best explained as the energy of our emotions.

If our emotional weather is trying to share the wisdom of our intuition, then one of the most powerful things we can do is expand our emotional vocabulary.

We must also do courageous and bold things like exploring not just our positive emotions, but also making space to hold our shadow side and the not so pretty emotions it offers.

Listening from the heart

One powerful tool for allowing our emotions to flow through us is the practice of heart-listening. I was introduced to this in many women's circles where we consciously created a sense of safety and deep connection.

Heart listening helps you create a pause in your day to cultivate an oasis of calm and self-connection that expands your capacity to receive divine wisdom. This practice is simple and effective. It's a physical act of breathing while placing your hand over your heart and noticing the thoughts and sensations that arise.

We can give ourselves this same gift and compassion by placing our hand over our physical heart space when we're consciously trying to move our emotions through and connect to our intuitive wisdom.

When we slow down and touch our heart space, we're connecting to the realm of love and self-compassion. The heart is vulnerable and sensitive, yet fiercely strong. In many ways, it's the ultimate source of our power.

Our intuition can be described by all these same qualities. Intuition is soft and yielding, yet fierce and determined. It yearns to help you and is always there, humming its song in the background, whether you're conscious of it or not.

When you give your attention to its existence and gently meditate on its steady rhythm, things slow down and unfurl with a surprising sense of ease and grace. You realize you are completely at home within yourself. A mist clears, and you see that all the answers you'd been seeking from out there can be accessed in this moment, from a point of stillness and embodied presence.

LEAN INTO YOUR EMOTIONS

Often, though our intention is to experience the radiance of our creative and visionary nature, we're met by a chorus of emotional gatekeepers that refuse us entrance to our inner sanctuary.

Just as you gain a greater sense of clarity about your vision, fear, anxiety, denial, or doubt come skipping along to throw you off the scent of your destiny. Having these emotions pop up doesn't necessarily mean you're off-course. It may just as well mean you're on the right track, but you've struck at the root of some deep-seated fears.

To avoid confusing your resistance and your intuition, it's important to understand the language of your feelings. We must be willing to name the emotions as they arise and dig deeper into the layers of wisdom and guidance they're presenting to us.

This is how to harness the power of our mind: to identify patterns and match up the information we've integrated long ago with the continual stream of our emotional life today.

Perhaps this is why so many visionaries find themselves drawn to books, courses, and articles on psychology and personal development. We know that if we can understand ourselves, we can bring our creative work to life.

If we learn to welcome all of our emotions and allow them to exist without pushing them away, we can consistently access the realm of our intuition. Feeling our emotions clears the way for intuition to rush in and show us what we most need to see or hear.

A significant aspect of healing in my mid thirties was a dedicated process of naming my emotions with greater detail. It took me years of practice and I had a lot of support on this journey. I would write and write in my journals until I could acknowledge my emotions and desires about even the smallest things, like which high chair to pick out for my son.

I acknowledged the emotions rising within me, even when I was afraid they were unwelcome to the people I was with or might lead to a feeling of judgment or disapproval in my relationships.

My writing practice was essential to this growth. When I translated the ever-flowing river of my emotional life into words and stapled it onto the paper with my pen and ink, I could see my thoughts with fresh and objective eyes. Because I'm energetically sensitive and open, I can easily become mixed up with other people's energy. I really couldn't tell what feelings belonged to me and which ones belonged to other people. This kept me perennially confused and stuck on my path.

Yet that feeling of being stuck, which I still have to work with, started to shake loose the more I wrote about my feelings around every decision I faced, big and small.

We all have this capacity to understand ourselves more deeply when we lean into our emotions and get curious about what they're trying to tell us. As you learn your own language, you'll be able to interpret your intuition with more ease and sensitivity. In turn, this will unlock all manner of wisdom, clues, and guidance to nurture your visionary awakening.

FOLLOW THE INNER COMPASS

Our intuition is always trying to help us find what's most true for our unique journey and will lead to the fulfillment of our soul's purpose. We will sway and teeter from right to left on this path, but ultimately our intuition is always guiding us forward.

A powerful skill for cultivating our intuition is to heighten the sensitivity of this emotional compass so we can access more and more of the information that lives within us.

When I was teaching Tarot courses, I always had my students review their deck of cards by intuitively sorting them into two piles. Picking the cards up, one at a time, they would notice their initial emotional response to the images and overall feeling of the card. If they had an open, positive, or neutral reaction, they placed the card on the 'yes' pile. If the card sparked a heavy, closed, or negative reaction, they placed that card on the 'no' pile.

After this quick initial sort, everyone reviewed the piles to find the five most potent cards they'd chosen from each stack. These cards would elicit a powerful or strong emotion, either positive or negative, and be set aside to work with later.

There are 78 cards in a deck of Tarot cards and from this exercise, each of us would choose just one or two of the most resonant and meaningful cards to represent the Sacred Yes and Sacred No cards in our deck.

The point of the exercise was not to create a rigid structure or attachment to these particular cards. The true benefit of this activity was to have an experience of absolute self-trust and acting on your intuition.

I often describe Tarot as a mirror, because the cards offer a way to see and understand yourself in new ways. So much of the world praises and celebrates us for pleasing others, whether or not it feels good for us to do so.

Essentially, this pattern leads to a world of millions upon millions of people who override their own intuition and don't believe they're allowed to follow their heart's messages and wisdom. Not only does this feel terrible, it also perpetuates self-doubt, suppresses our creativity, and hides our gifts from the world.

The antidote to these toxic patterns is to rebuild and reclaim our intuition from within. This example of practicing with a Tarot deck is just one way to cultivate this vital skill. When you give yourself permission to act on your initial reaction to each card, you're remembering what it feels like to know and follow your own inner compass.

Intuition keeps us supple, flexible, and fluid. Being intuitive means you're willing to be surprised, delighted, and unsure. Because uncertainty and not knowing is one of the few constants in life, when we're able to relax into this truth, we can transcend its perceived limitations.

Perhaps what I find most beautiful about turning towards our intuition is the way our entire body becomes a receptor and conduit for channeling information and wisdom. You can know something is right because of the way your arms tingle with awareness. Or you choose not to pursue a path because the pit of your stomach signals that this is deeply out of alignment with your purpose.

Intuition is a practice of letting go and stepping aside so our higher selves can help and support us in all ways. It is a force of good, a benevolent stream of love that's available to all of us and always has our best interest at heart.

Choosing the visionary path will invite you to sur-render your human love of plans and attachment to outcomes. If you choose to accept this invitation, it will open a doorway that leads to a garden of magic, alchemy, and wonder.

Yes, the quality of wonder is a guiding principle for your intuition. Wondering is to not-know, and to do so with a truly open heart that's willing to let in joy. When you can cultivate this curiosity from a place of love, you're on the path to a deeply intuitive life.

This is such a distinct energy from the relentless, persistent doubt of rational questioning most of us are accustomed to. We've become so serious in our lives that we attempt to treat our intuition like a scientific experiment. Driven by suspicion, we squeeze our intuition through tests and measurements to verify its validity and prove its truth.

But the power of intuition is nestled in its simplicity and playfulness. Intuition asks you to embrace your natural strengths of flexibility, fluidity, and delight. It gives you information that will lead you up the spiraling path of your soul's highest evolution and a way to live your life and express yourself that feels naturally vibrant and true.

Writing Invitations
to Awaken Intuition

When do you listen to your heart's wisdom?

How fluent are you in your emotional language?

What do you already know about the connection between your intuition and your body?

Do you embrace your emotions, or shy away from them?

Where is your inner compass pointing you right now?

BOUNDARIES

As you awaken your visionary voice, you must create a healthy container for this freshly activated energy flowing through your life. Boundaries are essential to your life and creative work; without them, your energy is easily diffused and your creative efforts can seem to dissolve into the mist.

Too many creative souls see boundaries as restrictive, when in fact they are vital for nourishing your visionary life. I had to learn the difference between suffocating limitations and healthy, nourishing boundaries. In the absence of healthy boundaries in my relationships and daily rhythms, I could never bring my dreams into full bloom.

The first step to creating healthy boundaries is to better understand what they are and why you need to cultivate and maintain them. A healthy boundary is a form of respect for yourself and others around you. They are built from a place of self-awareness about what does and doesn't work for you, and are upheld through clear and honest communication to others of what you will and will not do, accept, or tolerate.

Building this kind of boundary is deeply personal and requires a continual process that is never done. Boundaries are in a constant state of flow and change, just like everything else in life. As you awaken and befriend your visionary voice, it's perfectly natural for friction, frustration, or exhaustion to emerge around people, habits, or situations you've tolerated for years or even decades.

For example, you may be accustomed to sacrificing your creative time to meet the needs of others around you. It might be staying late at work, picking up all the slack with housework, or volunteering too much energy and attention to support other people with their problems or projects. This is an especially destructive pattern when those relationships offer you little support, and the dynamic is imbalance and extractive.

Once you awaken to how much of your energy is being drained, it's hard to unsee these depleting patterns. You might even feel a sense of grief or injustice that the world has been all too happy to take all that life force energy from you with little benefit in return. When you decide things have to change, you must go about the work of choosing yourself and saying no to as many of these demands as possible.

Please know that feathers may be ruffled in this process, but if you're able to slowly, steadily, and lovingly honor your new boundaries, eventually things can settle into a new normal. A normal that gives you the needed time and space to tend to your creative flame and share your voice, love, and wisdom with the world.

Our culture generally praises people for this so-called selflessness, particularly if you are a woman. As you become aware of your inner wisdom bubbling up and insisting on being shared, you'll also notice just how full your life is. Oddly enough, even if your life feels a little empty, as soon as you prioritize your writing and visionary voice, people in your life may notice the change and come up with unexpected needs or minor emergencies to demand your attention.

You will need to say no to others in order to say yes to yourself. You may need to decline offers or move on from friendships in order to create room in your heart, soul, and daily rhythm for your visionary voice to emerge.

Having struggled for decades with unhealthy boundaries and over-giving, I can tell you that even a small, subtle transformation in this area of your life is worth the effort. Your energy is not meant to be given away to other people without a loving flow of reciprocity.

I'd love to show you three simple yet potent ways to develop boundaries that will allow you to blossom on your path of awakening: time, energy, and attention.

Honor your time

Time is our most precious resource, a truly non-renewable gift we are each given. We may have different amounts of energy, health, or money, but we all have the same amount of time each day. This truth levels the playing field and unites us in our human experience.

Even though time is limited, I also believe it grows and expands when we bring our attention into the present moment. When I lead group writing exercises with a timer, I am always delighted to remember this again. Being absolutely present to the experience at hand, with no distractions, time slows down. Each second seems to grow longer and longer as I keep my attention firmly rooted in my writing.

I have three key beliefs around time boundaries that allow me to prioritize my writing, and to make the most of the minutes and hours I dedicate to my creative practice:

Very few people, if anyone at all, will offer me the time I most desire to feed my creativity.

When I make time for my writing, I'm not stealing it, I'm reclaiming it.

I only need a modest amount of time to feel creatively nourished.

VERY FEW PEOPLE, IF ANYONE AT ALL, WILL OFFER ME THE TIME I MOST DESIRE TO FEED MY CREATIVITY.

You can't evaluate your boundaries without recognizing exactly what season of life you're in, and who in your life depends on your time and energy. What agreements have you made about how you'll show up for the people in your life? How do you know when you've fulfilled those agreements?

No matter how well-meaning and loving the people are in your life, it's still rare for others to tell you to make time for yourself. In fact, I often hear people telling me I should make time for myself, without offering any tangible support to make that a reality.

For better or worse, the responsibility to prioritize your creative work falls to you. You must be the one who blocks out moments for your writing and protects them with a fierce sense of self-love and, dare I say it, survival. You might need to ask for help and support from friends and family and let them know how important your writing and creativity are for your emotional and spiritual wellbeing.

I'm writing this within a particular season of life as a mother of young children, wife, entrepreneur, and author. The hours in my day seem to wash away quickly as I juggle a merry-go-round of competing priorities and tasks. Each morning, I try to remind myself that the fullness of this moment will not last forever, and I may one day miss the bustle and noise of these long days.

If you're in a season filled with too many demands, you can take stock of where your energy is flowing and decide what can be let go for now. Take time to reflect on what will help you reclaim more time for your writing.

Who or what am I giving my time and energy to?

Who can I ask to support me in prioritizing my writing and creative work?

Am I prioritizing any projects that don't belong to me?

What time of day could be re-worked to make time for my writing?

WHEN I MAKE TIME FOR MY WRITING, I AM NOT STEALING IT, I AM RECLAIMING IT.

There was a popular quote going around in my women's circles that rubbed me the wrong way. It was Elizabeth Gilbert in her book *Big Magic* that wrote, "Traditionally, women have always made their art out of stolen materials and stolen time." But that statement is inherently flawed because it presumes that a woman's time doesn't belong to her. I decided then and there that I would have nothing to do with stealing time. Instead, I'm merely reclaiming what's rightfully mine when I choose to dedicate time to my writing and creativity.

Reclaiming your time is the only way to know yourself as an embodied writer. Meaning you are a person who writes regularly and often. You're not a person who talks about writing or wishes she was writing while gazing at a dusty pile of blank, empty notebooks.

What if you declared your creative time to be as essential as breathing, eating, or brushing your teeth? What if you decided that just because time for nurturing your creative self isn't handed over to you doesn't make it unnecessary or unimportant?

Tending, nourishing, and practicing your creativity is a worthy endeavor. Devoting your time to expressing yourself in joyful, creative ways is what brings you to life and fills you with love, compassion, and warmth to share with the people around you.

Dedicating your time to your creative expression is essential, not frivolous. When you arrive at this place of worthiness, of believing how much you deserve this time, you can finally uphold your boundaries and make time and space for your writing.

To reclaim is to retrieve what is lost. And my dear one, we are living in a time of great loss. The dominant culture has lost its connection to the Earth and the cycles of nature. What is lost is our right to slow down and to dream.

Yet again, choosing to write and reclaiming your time is a form of sacred resistance in a toxic culture that operates in a constant state of exploitation. You can become another voice that reminds us all that there is so much more to this human experience when we consciously slow down to know ourselves from the inside out.

I ONLY NEED A MODEST AMOUNT OF TIME
TO FEEL CREATIVELY NOURISHED.

The last point about your time boundaries is that you don't need endless hours for your creative practice to make an immediate and noticeable change in your life. When you're fully present, even five, 10, or 20 minutes of writing can hydrate your parched creative spirit.

I often imagine my creative heart as a little plant who needs to be watered regularly and lightly. If my roots dry out, I wilt. If I drift away from my writing practice for too long, I feel limp, disconnected, and disenchanted.

Ten minutes of writing can change your whole day. Twenty minutes is even better, but it's not necessary! When you become attached to an ideal scenario in which you have hours and hours of time to write, you may end up not writing at all. Writing and tending your visionary ideas needs to happen amidst the hubbub of your real life, with all of its complications, messiness, and competing priorities.

Start small and be consistent. Build up your stamina with tiny writing or creativity sessions, as many days a week as you can. The big work here is to uphold your own boundaries around this time you have reclaimed for your practice.

Treat yourself like your own highest priority. Honor yourself by showing up for your writing dates. See your time boundaries as an act of radical self-love that nourishes you from the roots up.

PROTECT YOUR ENERGY

Even when you carve out time for your writing, you may notice your energy levels are low or you feel fuzzy and unfocused. The first step in understanding how to cultivate healthy boundaries is to acknowledge that the ebb and flow of your creative energy is a very real aspect of our lives.

When I talk about energy, I mean your creative flow, your attention, and even your physical body. Visionaries are typically overflowing with creative energy, but for many of us, it spills out in a million directions and we're left with little to show for all of our efforts.

One of my children's teachers spoke about boundaries in such a beautiful way, describing them as the banks of a river. In a healthy river, the banks contain the flow of water without squeezing the current too tightly.

When the banks of the river close in and the boundaries become too tight and rigid, the river suffers. The water is squeezed too tightly and pressure builds up behind this blockage. A tremendous amount of energy and force is being generated in an effort to liberate the river's flow from this constriction. In this case, the water tears at the banks in a destructive way, eroding the land in order to force its way back to its desired state of flow.

In our creative life, this can happen if we set boundaries that are too tight, rigid, and restrictive. From the self-imposed pressure of a packed schedule or unrealistic deadlines, we find ourselves building up resentment and an almost painful experience of inner turmoil. The rigid boundaries we hoped would help us create more regularly end up generating unneeded struggle. It's like tying a tourniquet around your creative channel, and wondering why nothing seems to flow or feel pleasurable anymore when you sit down at your desk to dream and write.

The opposite experience of weakened boundaries is just as challenging. When our boundaries are too loose and lacking form, the water can't be held. It spills and floods over the plains. The flow may slow to a meager trickle, as most of the river's energy has been diverted into tiny puddles along the way. This typically looks like generating lots of work, but wondering what to do with it all. Or having lots of free time in your schedule, but still not sitting down with pen in hand to put your words on the page.

Without strong yet balanced boundaries to focus and concentrate our energy just enough, we're essentially powerless. We no longer know how to move ourselves forward and we feel either pinched off from our creativity, or hopelessly stretched thin and directionless.

Your creative energy is this water in the river. When it's contained by healthy boundaries, it can flow in a steady, sustainable way. The banks on either side hold this current firmly, yet with plenty of room for movement and flexibility. The river flows swift and clear, moving forward with confidence and direction. But if the boundaries are too restrictive or non-existent, this energy no longer functions effectively in your life.

In your daily life, this looks like giving yourself enough structure and space to have time for what matters most. You hold your boundaries and expectations with enough flexibility and compassion to accommodate the energy of spontaneity and the situations that will always emerge and demand your immediate attention.

Developing a keen sense of what drains your energy takes time. Quite often, it also requires an outside perspective or support. When we're so accustomed to living with an empty vessel, we can't even see how depleted we are.

One way to see your own energy patterns is to write about them. Spending some of your writing time reflecting on how your energy is flowing, or where it's being drained, is a fruitful way to identify and develop healthy energy boundaries.

- What caregiving or volunteer obligations are taking up your energy?

- What relationships tend to leave you feeling drained or depleted?

- Do you have creative projects that are taking your energy and need to be released?

- Are there times of the day when you feel the most energetically empty?

- Are there times of the day when you consistently have a good amount of energy?

- Can you remember specific times in your life when you felt energetically nourished? What were you doing, or what was different about that time compared to now?

As you get present to the flow of your energy, and become more aware of whether you're feeling energetically nourished or drained, you're gaining a valuable and useful tool. This level of self-awareness allows you to make powerful choices about where to invest your energy.

Think about where your energy really goes. In my experience, unless I'm being conscious about where I'm directing my energy, most of it goes to caregiving, worrying what other people think, wondering if I'm doing things right, and feeling anxious about what the future holds.

Just reading that list feels terrible in my body, but it also rings true. This is where my energy is consumed unless I'm consciously and purposefully telling it to fuel my creativity, my bigger visionary dreams, and most sacred relationships.

When my energy is being drained, my connection to my visionary voice feels thin. I can't hear myself think, let alone express my voice on the page. But when I'm tending to my energy, making sure I'm creatively, physically, and spiritually nourished, my voice thrives.

Each of us has a unique energetic composition. We all have different temperaments, energetic needs, and blueprints. The only way to know what works best for you is to pay attention to your own patterns.

Some of the more universal ways to refill your creative energy include time spent in nature, caring for your physical body, deep rest, and following your curiosity to learn new skills or embark on adventures.

Creating healthy boundaries around your energy is about protecting your time from the things that prevent you from tending to your essential needs. This all comes down to the choices we make, big and small, in our daily rhythms. You don't need to be perfect and you don't need to rearrange your entire life overnight.

Maybe you do need some sort of radical energy shift to create a massive reset. But for most of us, the changes can be small and subtle. They are little choices that add up over time. Like stepping away from your work for twenty minutes to go outside and sit next to a tree. Or taking fifteen minutes before bed to close your eyes, taking a few deep breaths, and consciously doing nothing so you can be still and present with your inner wisdom.

Guide your attention

In our modern experience, we have more demands placed on us than ever before. This requires us to hold even stronger boundaries than we needed even just a few decades ago. We're plagued with distractions and choices. Terms have been coined like 'decision fatigue' because of the sheer volume of input our attention is asked to handle on a daily basis.

Decision fatigue is a genuine phenomenon that can impair our quality of life, not to mention our creativity. Put simply, as your day goes on, making decision after decision, you eventually pay a price. Your decisions become less and less sensible, and each new decision becomes harder for your brain to process.

If you're ready to hear your inner voice with clarity and regularity, guiding your attention is an essential skill to cultivate. This is a soft, internal skill, but it's also a tangible and practical one. An immense amount of our attention is occupied by meeting our basic needs and navigating our physical environment.

By living in a cluttered space, for example, our minds are essentially processing each item in an endless cycle. If our digital environment is chaotic and disorganized, we waste time and energy trying to find things we've misplaced. When our phone has every single notification turned on across all our apps, this device robs us of our attention from morning until night.

Writing allows you to get clear on where you're directing your attention. Just taking the time to stop, slow down, and reflect on your current picture brings so much truth and clarity.

Here's where I like to start:

- What am I currently giving my attention to? (list anything and everything that comes to mind)

- What do I wish was receiving more of my attention?

- What is distracting me the most throughout the day?

- Make a list of as many things as possible that could minimize these daily distractions.

- Pick just one or two items from that list and try them today, or within the week.

Shifting your attention is simple, but it isn't easy. Even if you live in a minimalist house and have ample support in your life, you can still be distracted from what matters most. This is deep work, but it's a worthy endeavor that propels your journey of self-expression and awakening.

When I think about making a radical shift in boundaries, I turn to the words of Byron Katie, author of *A Mind at Home with Itself*. "Every no I say is a yes to myself. It feels right to me. People don't have to guess what I want or don't want, and I don't need to pretend."

Most creatives, heart-centered leaders and visionaries want to say yes to everything and everyone. You're a helper and a healer, so it almost feels like your job to drop what you're doing and race to someone else's side. Deep down, you likely know this isn't sustainable and leads to burnout.

What's the underlying force that leads to this habit? Do you fear that by saying no to others, you'll be unliked? Or maybe you'll be less spiritual, less worthy, or less enlightened?

Look at it from the other direction for a moment. If you have healthy boundaries and are willing to say no to things, your yes becomes that much more powerful and meaningful. Your time, energy, and attention can be directed to the people and endeavors that are most aligned with your talents, your desire, and your calling.

I want to acknowledge that this perspective is tangled up with many unjust things in our culture surrounding race, class, and gender. You can easily make the case that being able to truly guide your attention or say no to things isn't as simple when you're not a middle to upper class white man or white woman.

Still, I want to include this important concept because I believe we must help each other change these oppressive and extractive systems that make it feel impossible to say no or experience sovereignty over our attention.

If you take a step back and look at this landscape from 30,000 feet, what you'll see is a paradox of hyper-connectivity paired with loneliness, fatigue, and isolation. We're connected and interconnected through our modern forms of communication. I liken this new way of living as being covered in handles that people can pull on at any moment. We're simply more susceptible than ever to a cacophony of distracting voices, vices, and temptations.

Much of this information overload is pulling on and exploiting our core human survival instincts. We evolved to switch our focus to the most pressing or urgent task at hand in the case that such urgency was truly warranted. Quickly shifting our attention to respond to an attacking predator or an erupting volcano is an excellent thing. Switching focus to respond to each email as it floats in our inbox is not.

Most important is that as a visionary, we're tapped into a limitless realm of possibility and the connection to an overview of how everything fits together. We see all the options we could pursue and the paths we could take.

Translating that map of possibility into a set of focused actions to arrive at our designated outcome requires skill, practice, and the willingness to keep our attention focused on putting just one foot in front of the other.

While many people struggle with responsibilities, creative spirits are equally prone to suffer under the weight of possibility. You're passionate and fascinated by the world around you. You're curious and long to bring beautiful work into the world. You want to take every training and teach every workshop. If your time was as limitless as your appetite for life, you'd start a new business every morning.

Whether this bothers you a lot or just a little, to soar as a visionary, we must remind ourselves to come back to center and to stay on that one path that's spun around a thin yet powerful cord of golden light. Our visionary unfolding is centered around this thread, pulling us forward to our soul's calling.

If we keep reconnecting to this cord, again and again, we'll be able to bend time and experience more joy. This is the tether of our soul imprint that creates the greatest experience of satisfaction, fulfillment, and freedom.

We feel this golden thread of focused soul energy through our emotional guidance system and intuition. We feel it in our bodies and we know we're on our unique path when we sense that this filament is alive and thrumming with vibration within us.

You're hearing the call of your higher self, the aspect of you who is accessible in a realm where time and space are one. It's the aspect of yourself who has no future and no past and is offering you guidance on this lifetime journey.

This part of yourself has provided you a lifeline to follow, one that's quite clear if you're interested and willing to look for it. It's the luminous trail of breadcrumbs and clues that beckons you forward, whispering you the instructions you need to fulfill your highest purpose of this incarnation.

Writing Invitations
to Awaken Boundaries

Where are my edges in need of strengthening?

How am I pinching off my creative source with rigid boundaries?

Where is my energy diffused by a lack of healthy boundaries?

Which of my relationships model the healthy boundaries I want in my life?

How would I like to consciously create boundaries around my time, attention, and energy?

ENOUGHNESS

You are enough. Your ideas, your voice, your truth, your creativity. It is all enough.

The fear that what you have to say is not enough is one of the biggest blocks to expressing your voice, creativity, and wisdom. There you are, filled with ideas and inspiration, yet feeling blocked and separated from bringing this goodness out into the world. Your writing, books, and creations remain a mirage, floating somewhere between a dream and a reality.

The visionary voice yearns to be heard, it tugs at your sleeve asking to be acknowledged and liberated. Meanwhile, another part of you craves safety and abhors the risk of speaking up or being seen. Gripped with fear, your mouth remains tightly shut, your voice is stifled.

As with so many aspects of awakening, the only way to work through this inner tangle is by leaning in with gentle curiosity. What are the roots of your unique fear of sharing your voice and speaking your truth? We each have a unique constellation of experiences that grows into that aching sense that who you are and what you have to offer just isn't good enough.

One of my most tenaciously rooted fears is a deep, gnawing feeling that it's dangerous and unacceptable to share my ideas until they're perfect and beyond reproach. Perfectionism is a bramble with ragged thorns designed to keep you safely in place. One move toward your desires and dreams and those barbs dig right in. You wonder, is it really worth it to move forward? Is it worth it to tear out of this overgrown thicket?

I invite you to explore what those brambles look like for you. For each of us, they overlap and intertwine because so many of them are based in our culture,

our shared experiences, and the collective uncon-
scious. Many of these fears have been carried down
through generations, trauma and beliefs that become
encoded in our very DNA.

Usually, the result of these patterns is resistance to
speaking up, standing out, and allowing our whole
self to be heard and seen. You respond by deciding
that if you're going to expose yourself to criticism,
you need to water your ideas down or only share a
tiny sliver of the picture of your beliefs.

Deep down, you're driven by a belief that says I'm
not enough, my ideas aren't good enough, and what
I have to say isn't perfect enough.

Enough, enough, enough.

Seeing ourselves as not enough is a falsehood we
learn to carry, the result of a society that ranks, sorts,
and compares us to one another. After a lifetime of
being graded, judged, and evaluated, we learn to
censor, regulate, and constrict ourselves. We
become the harshest critic of our voice and our ideas.
No one has to even tell us anymore to be quiet or
fade into the background.

Exploring this inner construct through writing can help you slice through the tight restraints of self-censorship. Within the safety of your journal, you can run wild with your thoughts and give light to your beliefs. You can escape the confines of self-judgment.

The world is wild and imperfect. Everything changes, everything follows the natural cycles of birth, death, and rebirth. We are messy and wondrous.

Here is the full truth: you're more than enough. You're a spark of perfect beauty, a reflection of the infinite cosmos in flesh and bone.

Let's not forget the high price we pay for silencing ourselves because we believe we're not enough. The world misses out on our magic. We slowly decay from the inside out with these beautiful gems stuck inside us.

DISMANTLING THE WEB
OF SELF-CENSORSHIP

Ultimately, to believe you are enough is to accept your inherent completeness. Who told you that somehow you're lacking the wisdom or resources to bring your gifts into the world? When did you come to believe that who you are and what you have to say isn't good enough or smart enough?

Living in a constant state of muffling your inner voice erodes your vibrancy and confidence. You know there is another way. This part of you isn't concerned in the least about what others may think of her. Your voice has a fierce desire to be heard, and the path of awakening is simply to soften all the ways in which you've sealed this power in a tight, dark bundle within you.

I understand how heavy the expectations are that are placed on us from such an early, tender age. We're thrown into a system of impossible duality: we are good or bad, a success or a failure, a winner or a loser. Navigating this feels terrible to our bodies because the very root of us understands how completely un-human this structure is.

Your Visionary Voice knows, beyond all doubt, that we exist within an unbroken circle. Everything cycles back on itself, like the snake eating its tail in the image of the magical Ourobos.

Black and white thinking exacerbates the anxiety and fear that we won't measure up, and then our reputation will be forever tarnished. Once we've been put in that box, the one labeled FAILURE, we don't think anyone will care what we have to say, ever again.

The work of dismantling this matrix of self-censorship may continue for your lifetime, because the world is so steeped in this perspective. The patterns are strong and like to grow back.

But this scenario isn't the truth, and your visionary voice knows it. When you're rooted in your enoughness, there is a lightness to your being, a playful quality you bring to everything you do.

You can care deeply and express yourself without being stuck, stagnant, or rigid. A courageous voice of enoughness is good friends with an ear that listens with compassion and an open heart to other people. The quality of enoughness spills out of you and into other people, who breathe a deep sigh of relief and gratitude that someone else has given them permission to simply BE.

Almost any writing practice can become a portal to self-expression without self-censorship. However, approaching the page with a clear and focused intention to let yourself be truly free is when the real magic can happen.

Pick up the pen and let yourself rant. Let yourself feel, cry, rage, and moan. Complain about how unfair it is that you live in a culture that tells you to keep your thoughts to yourself, or tells you that who you are isn't enough.

Then harvest that energy you've tapped into, the passion and fiery conviction, and channel it into your creative power.

These reflection questions can help…

> *How have you already started to unravel this dysfunctional pattern within yourself?*

> *Make a list of all the times you have spoken up and told the truth. How did those moments feel?*

> *What part of you has been hearing the call to use your voice to help yourself and others?*

LET IT BE EASY

Another flavor of believing you're not good enough is to continually avoid sharing your creations because you think they're not done yet. Too often, this is connected to a cultural acceptance of struggle that prevents us from easily moving through the world with wonder and grace.

I've felt this as a need to prove myself worthy by wearing a badge of struggle to justify the audacity of speaking up. When you're committed to struggle, you're easily swept away in a sea of self-criticism. It might come in endless waves of thoughts like:

> *I don't have enough degrees to talk about this idea.*

> *I haven't spent enough time editing this poem to share it with anyone else.*

> *My ideas will come out jumbled and laughable when I'm speaking to the group.*

> *The only way to get this done is to sacrifice my health and relationships.*

But what if you're afraid to let it be easy? What if your truth and vision feel so big that you tumble into fear and believe it's going to be a painful process to bring it to life?

As a visionary, you can see the whole picture of whatever mission or purpose you've been called to create. Your voice can paint the scene in all its glorious details when everything has come together in perfect alignment.

This vision will only become concrete over time, as you take one tiny step, followed by another. With big ideas, you may be tempted to dismiss these tiny steps as insignificant, as not enough. This is where too many of us get off track and stop ourselves from allowing our true voice to find its way into the real world.

Instead, what if you celebrated these tiny steps and applauded yourself for your tenacity and conviction? What if you let yourself feel the delicious experience of growth, momentum, and expansion that comes from manifesting the boldest version of your voice and vision?

The little steps might be simple and easy. But this doesn't make them less important. In fact, this is where the magic happens. Each baby step is a portal that allows more of your truth to emerge and paves the way for even wilder waves of imagination to flood forth.

Let it be easy, let it be enough.

Contentment over striving

Enoughness is the antidote to the striving, pushing, and imbalanced dynamic of patriarchy in the Western world.

The opposite of enoughness is the hungry ghost within us, as described in Buddhism. This is the enormous mouth of hunger within us that can never be satiated. No matter how much praise, validation, money, or material possessions we acquire, there's no ultimate satisfaction or contentment. No matter what you feed the mouth, it remains a source of hunger and yearning.

In the pursuit of enough as an external state, we become trapped on a treadmill of everlasting discontent. The way we can cultivate enoughness is to shift our attention within and consciously cultivate a practice of appreciation and radical acceptance.

When we relate to 'not enough' as 'something's wrong', we continue feeding the hungry ghost. Yet if we were to stop fighting that ghost, and stop trying to feed it with desperate, hurried attempts to fill the un-fillable void, we can shift onto a new road paved with peace.

We can choose an alternative path that's built upon the foundations of self-compassion and self-love. It's possible to love the hungry, needy part of ourselves, with its endless longing for more. We can remind each other that attempting to fill this void will never bear the fruit of true peace or fulfillment.

Where we veer off track with this is by confusing our desire for growth with our desire for more. In Western culture, we're obsessed with prosperity and material displays of wealth and abundance. But without a holistic view of what true nourishment and fulfillment mean to us, we're attempting to find comfort by sitting on a one-legged stool. Trying to do this requires a huge amount of effort and it's uncomfortable on some level, no matter what we try. We can never truly rest or relax.

Money and material goods are only one facet of abundance and enoughness. Our wealth on paper isn't the total picture, nor is it a very good indication of our holistic and spiritual well-being.

When you chase money for money's sake, it's easy for your focus to drift away from your true purpose. I've adopted the wise words of Tosha Silver from *It's Not Your Money* as a mantra for how to trust the flow of abundance, but you can apply it to just about anything: "Let what wants to come, come. Let what wants to go, go. If it is mine, it will stay. If not, whatever is better will replace it."

The quality of enoughness is also confused with our inherent, divinely appointed self-worth. Our worth is infinite, a reflection of the unfathomable and endless expanse of the Universe and the Source of all Love and Life.

You don't need to do anything to be worthy, valuable, or enough. You're born whole and complete, deserving in every way, and this worthiness doesn't diminish over time. It's always there as a fundamental truth of who you are.

Unfortunately, the society most of us grew up in has traded trust and connection for fear and separation. Our culture is designed to thrive on comparison, judgment, tribalism, and dysfunctional competition.

This is why so many creative voices, who know at a deep soul level that this is a harmful and false paradigm, have struggled to thrive in these conditions.

We're not raised in a fertile soil that nourishes the manifestation of our visionary dreams. Enoughness must be a revolution that begins with you.

When you stand in the truth of your enoughness, you're anchored in the full source of your power. If you can live and speak from this place of enoughness, the vibration and resonance of your voice is so magnetic, others can't help but take notice. When you're aligned with the energy of your own enoughness, your blind spots dissolve and room is made for clarity to emerge.

You are already enough, so you've likely experienced this sensation at different times in your life. You felt lit up from within. Quietly peaceful. Fiercely clear yet deeply calm. You felt a complete sense of being at home in your body, mind, and spirit.

You radiated a feeling of integrity and connectedness to your true self that was palpable to those around you. Perhaps people reacted to you differently in these moments. Or you felt a sense of absolute clarity in your thought and speech, as if your truth was easily tumbling out with potent aliveness.

When you're present to your enoughness, your energetic field expands and the influence of your message is amplified. It reaches farther and farther into the world, catalyzed by your grounded alignment with a deeper source of self-love and self-acceptance.

You are not too much

I can vividly remember my second-grade classroom, and the moment in my life when I learned that my enthusiasm was too big and too much. I raised my hand to answer the teacher's question, so filled with excitement to share myself that I couldn't help but wiggle my feet and puff out my chest. Bursting to speak, I was using every ounce of will to restrain myself as best I could.

Yet in the face of this exuberance, my teacher, a woman in her 40s, told me to wait outside the classroom because I was too excited. I froze instantly with shame and embarrassment. I stood outside the door, alone in the hallway, and vowed I would never let myself be shunned like this again. I can still feel the heat in my cheeks as I struggled to process my anger and guilt.

The lesson my soul learned was that I was far too much for this world. If I was going to navigate life successfully, I would have to tone it down. To pretend I didn't care and that I wasn't actually that excited about anything. I would need to mask my intelligence and my fire in order to fit in with whatever this culture was that I'd been born into.

And so it goes with us, the visionary voices. At some point along the way, you were given this same message. You are TOO MUCH.

Forever after, we will hide some or all of our fullness. Even if it's just the corners of ourselves, just 10% of our essence tucked away in some well-hidden treasure chest. We know it's not safe to bring everything we've got to the table.

This is the flip side of enoughness, the idea that we're actually far too much. Too smart, connected, intuitive, bossy, opinionated, and demanding.

We want too much and our desire for more is embarrassing. Again and again, we're reminded that our bright, effervescent spirit needs to be masked and blend in with the scenery a whole lot better.

As I continually walk with not-enoughness on my own creative journey, I penned a short poem of sorts, or perhaps more of a mantra. These are reminders that soothe my heart when I notice myself shying away from my inner voice.

I am safe here in this space.

I can bring my whole self into the room.

It's safe to be in my body.

I accept the fullness of my inner radiance

I welcome my wholeness,
I embrace my capacity to shine.

I move through the world with
fire, love, and grace.

May I remember the brilliance that resides
in the inner sanctuary of my soul, the seat
of love and connection to all that is.

Writing Invitations
to Awaken Enoughness

*Why do you believe that you're too much
or not enough?*

When did you decide that you were too much?

*When do you first remember deciding you'd have to
hide your truth to fit in?*

*How does this pattern keep repeating itself in your
life now?*

*What terrible thing would happen if you shared
your whole self?*

*What wonderful thing would happen if you
spoke your truth?*

INTEGRATION

I love myself enough to be

patient with my process

INTEGRATION

Awakening your visionary voice is not a process with a clear beginning, middle, and end. No, there is no ultimate completion to this experience. There is no badge, certificate, or finish line that you'll cross to know with certainty that you've arrived.

Whatever is awakening within you will continue to do so as long as you allow the process to continually unfurl. Because of this, your awakening may feel like a falling-apart or an unraveling. Perhaps coming undone and seeing things with fresh eyes is exactly what needs to happen for you?

In any transformational process, it's vital to have resources and tools for the ongoing process of integration. Integration is part of the transformational cycle that doesn't receive the attention it deserves. I offer these tools to carry alongside your creative rituals and writing sessions.

Integration looks like shifting your perspective or forming a new connection, and then consciously making space to integrate your new awareness or wisdom. Particularly if you experience a more pronounced or intense realization, integration practices allow you to more effectively metabolize and digest what you've experienced.

In my own practice of Wild Embodied Writing, I primarily turn to physical practices that nourish and settle my mind and body before and after I write. This includes drumming, singing, walking, stretching, and deep breathing. All of these activities engage my physical body in a replenishing way, and work to effectively soothe and regulate my nervous system.

All change asks us to grow and expand to become a container for a bigger perspective or a wider awareness. Stretching must be done with mindfulness and care. You don't want to force your transformation, only to snap something fragile that ends up requiring even deeper healing.

What might transformational integration look like for you? Consider what you already know works well for you to replenish and nurture your feeling of being grounded and aligned. My experience has shown that a combination of movement, rest, and writing helps me to process and integrate while I dismantle old patterns and build new ones.

This list is just a starting point to inspire you to create your own array of integration resources and exercises:

- Stretching

- Dancing

- Walking

- Twisting

- Qi Gong / Tai Chi

- Singing

- Drumming

- Laughing

- Breathwork / Pranayama / Breath of Fire

- Yin Yoga

- Sauna / Cold plunging

- Meditation

Skipping the integration step makes it more challenging to sustain the wisdom that is emerging within you. Without taking time to allow the full magic of your awakening to circulate through your system, your process will feel lopsided and frayed. You might become confused rather than clear, overwhelmed rather than inspired.

Beyond the physical integration of embodying your visionary voice, there is the outward step of sharing your voice. This also requires a gentle approach, so you can slowly expand your comfort with speaking up, being seen, and communicating your visionary wisdom.

One of the first visionary truths shared in this book is that everything you do is driven by a desire for love and connection. You get to decide how you will form these connections. You can choose to focus on showing up differently in your immediate, intimate circles of family or friends, or heed a call to take on a larger stage.

Thinking of your life as a series of expanding circles of safety and belonging is a way to test the experience of sharing your voice without overdoing it. You decide on the scope and scale that's aligned for you and your soul work.

Changing how you show up and use your voice is a vulnerable act, and a brave one as well. You may be quite comfortable speaking to large groups, but avoid speaking the truth to those you're closest to. Which makes perfect sense, as it can feel riskier to change or shift within those sacred relationships. Or perhaps you're able to be honest and vulnerable when it's just you and a few friends having tea, but the idea of being heard by a large group of strangers induces immediate panic.

Notice where your comfort level is right now, and contemplate what else you want to try to fully embrace your visionary work. If you stay open and curious, the answers to these questions will naturally reveal themselves to you. As the direction becomes clear, your next invitation is to lovingly take risks and step outside of your comfort zone.

This is where you'll have to decide how to take risks that are the right-size for you. For your personality, your nervous system, and your dreams. I believe you must honor who you are and where you are at this very moment. I don't believe in pushing yourself past your limits in ways that are destabilizing or make you feel ungrounded.

A repeatable pattern forms: you stretch yourself and expand your capacity for courageously honoring your inner voice, then rest, recover, and integrate your experience. I see this stage of awakening as the development of embodied discernment. You trust your body to show you what it needs to be filled with the full potency of your voice and awakening wisdom. You must choose what works best for you. You must decide how and when you're going to use your voice in service to your visions, dreams, and desires.

I offer these mantras as a way to stay centered within yourself on this journey:

I am the expert on me

I honor and trust my own limits

I love myself enough to be patient with my process

You are here to do this work for a lifetime, whatever that creative, inspiring, and visionary work may be. You are not meant to burn out, you're meant to smolder. You are here to burn bright, strong, and true for decades.

This world needs you like never before. We need your story, your talents, and your gifts. We need your visionary voice.

You're here for a reason

You have something to share

It's time to do what you're here to do

ACKNOWLEDGMENTS

With deep reverence, I acknowledge that I live and work in the unceded Pocumtuc land of the Kwinitekw Valley and neighboring indigenous nations, the Nipmuc and the Wampanoag to the east, the Mohegan and Pequot to the South, the Mohican and Nonotuck to the west, and the Abenaki to the North.

I offer my work within a deep commitment to create a more diverse, equitable, and inclusive community of writers, entrepreneurs, and experts, and build programs, offerings, and resources so that people of different ethnicities, genders, cultures, belief systems, class backgrounds, ages, abilities, and sexual orientations have genuine and equal opportunities to thrive.

At each step of my creative unfurling, I have been supported and loved by countless kindred spirits. Friends, family, soul mates, clients, and colleagues have each contributed to the blossoming of this book.

I thank the women in my life, who form a circle of fierce courage and love that keeps me anchored and thriving. Please know that ALL of you are in my heart every day, and this list is far from comprehensive. Nicola, for your unbound magic. Melinda for your ceaseless encouragement and friendship. Wendy, for your fire and empathy. Dana, for your radiance and inspiration. Elaina for holding my vulnerability with care and offering your own writerly prowess to refine my thoughts, both in life and on the page.

To my ancestors, whose ingenuity, resilience, and determination made my existence and work possible.

For my partner, whose steadfast support allows me to soar. And for my beautiful boys, who remind me that the path of awakening is to make the world as beautiful as possible for them.

ABOUT THE AUTHOR

Leah Kent is a writer and book coach who supports wisdom keepers and visionaries to bring their books to life. She supports these heart-centered creatives, experts, and entrepreneurs to write and self-publish books that clarify their message, establish their thought-leadership, and expand their impact and visibility.

Through her Wild Embodied Writing method and community, Leah has helped dozens of clients unlock their most aligned self-expression and bring their message into the world. These writers are driven by a deep sense of purpose and passion for helping and healing, and work in professions such as psychology, somatic healing, mental health and wellbeing, spirituality, and creativity.

To learn more about Leah's work, visit **LeahKent.net** or connect on **Instagram @leahkentco**

Printed in Great Britain
by Amazon

61015971R00109